S0-CFR-929

POWER FACTOR SPECIALIZATION
Chest&Arms

PETER SISCO AND JOHN LITTLE

authors of *POWER FACTOR TRAINING*

CB
CONTEMPORARY BOOKS

Library of Congress Cataloging-in-Publication Data

Sisco, Peter.
     Power factor specialization : chest & arms / Peter Sisco and
John Little.
        p.   cm.
     Includes bibliographical references and index.
     ISBN 0-8092-2829-7
     1. Bodybuilding—Physiological aspects.   2. Arm exercises.
3. Chest.   I. Little, John R., 1960–   .   II. Title.
RC1220.W44S56   1999
613.7′11—dc21   98-46770
                                                        CIP

Cover design by Todd Petersen
Cover photograph copyright © 1998 Kurt Gerber
Interior design by Hespenheide Design
Interior photographs by Mike Spencer

Published by Contemporary Books
A division of NTC/Contemporary Publishing Group, Inc.
4255 West Touhy Avenue, Lincolnwood (Chicago), Illinois 60646-1975 U.S.A.

Copyright © 1999 by Peter Sisco and John Little
All rights reserved. No part of this book may be reproduced, stored in a retrieval
system, or transmitted in any form or by any means, electronic, mechanical,
photocopying, recording, or otherwise, without the prior written permission of
NTC/Contemporary Publishing Group, Inc.
Printed in the United States of America
International Standard Book Number: 0-8092-2829-7

99 00 01 02 03 04 VL 18 17 16 15 14 13 12 11 10 9 8 7 6 5 4 3 2 1

This book is dedicated to every person who is willing to apply reason, logic, and the scientific method to discover truth. From Empedocles to Galileo to, perhaps, the person holding this book, these are the people who insist on evidence, eschew dogma, help discover new knowledge, and thereby improve the lives of all.

PETER SISCO

To John Grimek and Benjamin Little, one who blazed new trails by leading a fulfilling, exciting, and productive life, and one who is about to.

JOHN R. LITTLE

Caution: This program involves a systematic progression of muscular overload that leads to the lifting of extremely heavy weights. As a result, a proper warm-up of muscles, tendons, ligaments, and joints is mandatory at the beginning of every workout.

Warning: As this is a very intense program, it requires both a thorough knowledge of proper exercise form and a base level of strength fitness. Although exercise is very beneficial, the potential for injury does exist, especially if the trainee is not in good physical condition. Always consult with your physician before beginning any program of progressive weight training or exercise. If you feel any strain or pain when you are exercising, stop immediately and consult your physician.

Other Books by Peter Sisco and John Little

Static Contraction Training: Gain Up to 25 Pounds of Pure Muscle Mass in Ten Weeks

The Golfer's Two-Minute Workout: Add 30 Yards to Your Drive in Six Weeks

Power Factor Training: A Scientific Approach to Building Lean Muscle Mass

Contents

1 **Why You Need This Book**   1
It's About Progress   1
The Benefits   2
Compare Two Workouts   4
The Failure of Conventional Bodybuilding Methodology   6
Why Specialize?   8

2 **Power Factor Training Fundamentals**   11
What Is a Power Factor?   11
Analyzing by Power Factor   12
Your "Sweet Spot"   15
Beta Strength and the Power Index   18
Two Ways to Grow   21
Sisco's Laws of Bodybuilding   24
Intensity vs. Duration   27
Recovery   27
Full Range vs. Strongest Range   32
How Muscle Tissue Is Stimulated   34
The Birth of the Overload Principle   34
Enter the Power Factor   37
Specialization vs. Generalization   39

3 **The Muscles of the Chest**   43
The Chest—Anatomy and Physiology   43
Chest Exercises   44

4 **The Muscles of the Arms**   63
The Triceps—Anatomy and Physiology   64
Triceps Exercises   64
The Biceps—Anatomy and Physiology   80

Biceps Exercises   80
The Forearms—Anatomy and Physiology   102
Forearm Exercises   104

5 Rating the Chest Exercises   121
What Are We Trying to Prove This Time?   121
Exercising to Failure   122
Rating the Exercises   123
Chest Exercises   124

6 Rating the Arm Exercises   137
Triceps Exercises   137
Biceps Exercises   148
Forearm Exercises   160

7 Specialized Chest Routines   171
High Alpha Strength Chest Workouts   172
High Beta Strength Chest Workouts   175
Record Keeping   177

8 Specialized Arm Routines   179
High Alpha Strength Triceps Workouts   179
High Beta Strength Triceps Workouts   182
Record Keeping   184
High Alpha Strength Biceps Workouts   184
High Beta Strength Biceps Workouts   185
High Alpha Strength Forearm Workouts   186
High Beta Strength Forearm Workouts   188
The Winning Combination   188
Frequency of Workouts   189

9 Tracking Your Progress   191
Keeping Track of Your Numbers   192
Engineering Your Next Workout   195
Progress Graph   197
Understanding Recovery   200
Blank Performance Record and Exercise Performance Record   202

10 Questions and Answers   207

Index   243

POWER FACTOR SPECIALIZATION
Chest&Arms

Why You Need This Book

IT'S ABOUT PROGRESS

We have never ceased to be amazed by the willingness of body-builders and those seeking to increase their health and fitness levels to accept as truth unproved edicts that have endured throughout decades. It does not follow that because a bodybuilder happens to possess, say, a massively developed arm that he knows the first thing about productive exercise. Given the role that genetics play in the bodybuilding equation, coupled with the rampant abuse of growth drugs, the odds are that the advice that most "champions" or genetic freaks can provide you is useless at best, and at worst a threat to your well-being.

Bodybuilders, particularly those seeking to improve the size of specific body parts (hence the need for the books in this Power Factor Specialization series), willingly train for months and even years with little or nothing to show in the way of progress. The reason, in large part, is that none of them seems to know what he can realistically expect in the way of results from workout to workout and that many foolishly believe the advertising hype that accompanies exercise equipment, nutritional supplements, or the training method allegedly employed by a champion bodybuilder. Not knowing what to expect, who's telling the truth, or even what the truth of the matter is, such bodybuilders often waste years of their lives frantically trying one product or method promoted in the various muscle magazines and by the champion du jour after another.

The good news we have for you in the Power Factor Specialization series is that unproductive workouts are now a thing of the past. With this book, you have in your possession the well-settled results of research testing on the most popular exercises—and equipment—employed by bodybuilders in their quest to develop bigger, stronger chests, biceps, triceps, and forearms. We have taken the guesswork out of what works and the degree to which it works and then quantified the best muscle-building exercises numerically so that you will know at a glance which exercises are truly the best for adding serious muscle size to your chest and arms on a progressive basis. You can then combine those exercises into specialized routines to ensure maximum muscle stimulation each and every workout.

Power Factor Specialization: Chest & Arms is going to prove something else that will startle bodybuilders, strength and conditioning coaches, personal trainers, and exercise physiologists. We have scientifically established that many of the exercises that these individuals have held up as the bedrock of common strength-training programs are so grossly inefficient that they are almost a complete waste of time. This includes exercises performed on some of the most expensive equipment made.

Along the way we will also explode a few myths regarding the supposed superiority of certain machine exercises and reveal why strong-range training is—and will remain—the most productive way to train your muscles if serious gains in strength and size are your goals.

THE BENEFITS

Power Factor Training was designed to yield a threefold dividend:

1. to promote the highest possible gains in muscular size and strength
2. to measure the quantity of muscular output required for each workout in order to induce those gains
3. to determine and monitor each individual's innate adaptability to exercise, so that his progress will be consistent and he can avoid overtraining

The supreme importance of muscular overload in bodybuilding has been established beyond question, both in the lab and by bodybuilders in the gym throughout the past five decades.

Specialization allows you to provide concentrated growth and recovery energy to your chest and arm muscles only.

Different training systems have delivered varying degrees of over-load and, hence, varying degrees of muscle-growth stimulation.

However, until Power Factor Training came on the scene in 1993, there existed no training method that integrated a precise method of measuring these varying degrees of overload and their effects on the muscle-growth process systematically. Now, body-builders in over fifty-eight countries are using Power Factor Training to achieve all three of these objectives simultaneously, and the results that it produces have been absolutely astounding, even to those who are very experienced in bodybuilding.

COMPARE TWO WORKOUTS

Let us suppose that a trainee goes into a gym and wants to know what is the best way to train his chest. He's lucky: on this day two individuals—both of them champion bodybuilders—are about to train their chests. The man pulls out his notebook and secretly records the particulars of each man's chest workout with an eye toward later adopting the workout program he feels is the most effective.

The first champion begins his chest routine. He starts with 4 sets of bench presses to get things rolling. He does 1 set of 15 reps at 135 pounds, 1 set of 10 reps at 155 pounds, 1 set of 8 reps at 175 pounds, and finally 1 set of 3 reps at 200 pounds.

Next up for the champ is 4 sets of incline presses using 105 pounds for 12 reps, 135 pounds for 10 reps, 145 pounds for 9 reps, and 155 pounds for 8 reps. From there it's on to dumbbell flies for 3 sets of 12 reps with a pair of 45-pound dumbbells. Our curious friend notes that champion #1's chest workout took him 30 min-utes to complete. All in all, it was a pretty conventional body-building workout, the kind you see performed in virtually any bodybuilding gym on almost any day of the week.

The man sharpens his pencil as the second champion gets set to perform his chest routine. This champion, however, selects but one chest exercise, barbell bench presses on a flat bench, and bangs out 6 sets of 30 repetitions with 155 pounds in a span of 10 minutes. His workout over, champion #2 leaves the gym.

Now, however, our bodybuilding trainee is left with vexing questions: Which champion stimulated more muscle growth? And more important, how can he know? The answer to these queries forms the thesis of this book. The only way to answer this man's questions lies not in the crude gauges of feel and instinct, as some bodybuilding theorists (and not a few personal trainers, by the way) would have you believe. Nor is it to be found in that vague concept known as *holistic training*. He can find the answers to these questions only when he discovers just how muscle growth is stimulated.

After some serious research, our trainee would learn that muscle growth, as explained in our book *Power Factor Training: A Scientific Approach to Building Lean Muscle Mass* (Contemporary Books, 1997), can be stimulated only by having a muscle perform more work (that is, lift more weight for more repetitions) in a given unit of time than it did previously. There are no other considerations in this equation. If your muscles performed more work (that is, lifted more weight on a pounds-per-minute basis), then growth will have been stimulated. If they didn't, not only was growth not stimulated, but the indications are that you haven't recovered from your previous workout and would have benefited from putting off your workout for another few days.

Still, the question remains: Which of the two outlined workouts stimulated the greater muscle growth? The answer lies in computing the Power Factor of the two workouts. The Power Factor is determined by dividing the total weight lifted (weight × reps × sets) by the total time of the workout itself. The more weight lifted on a pounds-per-minute basis, the greater the Power Factor and, hence, the greater the muscle-growth stimulation. Now our trainee has a way to measure the productiveness of each of the champions' workouts. Let's look at his data:

Champion #1's Chest Workout				
Exercise	**Sets**	**Reps**	**Weight**	**Total Weight**
Bench presses	1st	15	135 lb.	2,025 lb.
	2nd	10	155 lb.	1,550 lb.
	3rd	8	175 lb.	1,440 lb.
	4th	3	200 lb.	600 lb.
Incline presses	1st	12	105 lb.	1,260 lb.
	2nd	10	135 lb.	1,350 lb.
	3rd	9	145 lb.	1,305 lb.
	4th	8	155 lb.	1,240 lb.
Dumbbell flys (2 × 45 lb.)	1st	12	90 lb.	1,080 lb.
	2nd	12	90 lb.	1,080 lb.
	3rd	12	90 lb.	1,080 lb.

Total Weight: 13,970 pounds (weight 3 reps 3 sets)
Total Time: 30 minutes
Power Factor: 466 lb./min. (total weight ÷ total time)

Champion #2's Chest Workout

Exercise	Sets	Reps	Weight	Total Weight
Bench presses	1st	30	155 lb.	4,650 lb.
	2nd	30	155 lb.	4,650 lb.
	3rd	30	155 lb.	4,650 lb.
	4th	30	155 lb.	4,650 lb.
	5th	30	155 lb.	4,650 lb.
	6th	30	155 lb.	4,650 lb.

Total Weight: 27,900 pounds
Total Time: 10 minutes
Power Factor: 2,790 lb./min.

Now our aspiring bodybuilder has the answers to his questions in black and white. Champion #2's workout stimulated far and away more muscle growth. In every aspect, Champion #2's chest training was more productive. It exceeded the total weight lifted of Champion #1's workout by almost double the amount of muscular output (that is, 27,900 vs. 13,970 pounds) and, more important, the Power Factor was a staggering 2,324 pounds per minute higher than Champion #1's.

Making your muscles move that much more weight over a given unit of time imposes an incredible demand on the muscles and the systems that supply them. Because of the magnitude of this demand, your body increases its muscle mass stores in order to guard against future stressors of like severity. This divested of all its academic trappings is the simple truth of how muscle growth is stimulated not only in your pectoral muscles but in every muscle group in your body.

THE FAILURE OF CONVENTIONAL BODYBUILDING METHODOLOGY

Without making these calculations, it would be impossible for anyone to determine which of the two workouts was the more productive. In fact, we would have had to rely on "feel," muscle soreness, outright guessing, or some other arbitrary index of progress. Such a manner of monitoring your results is, of course, tantamount to having no way of monitoring your results. This is where Power Factor Training makes its most radical break from conventional weight training. Most bodybuilders in the gym train with absolutely no conception of how long it takes them to complete their exercises. Can you imagine an athlete in any other sport training so haphazardly? That said, we should point out that there exists no magic formula for sets, reps, and weights—at least not one that applies across the board. Nevertheless, with Power Factor Training there is finally a method that allows each individual to find his own.

Prior to Power Factor Training's arrival on the bodybuilding scene, there existed no objective gauge by which to accurately measure the effectiveness of a bodybuilding exercise. In fact, each

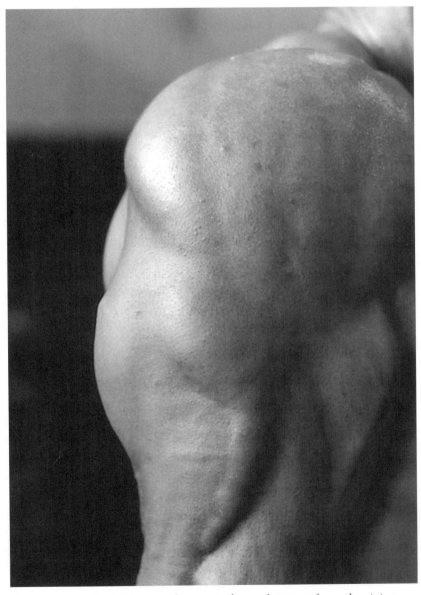

The advantage afforded by specialization is that such intense focused training allows the trainee to maximally stimulate a lagging body part into new levels of growth—without running the risk of overtraining.

exercise was said to be of equal value, owing to the fact that most believed that you have to change your exercises frequently in order to prevent the muscles from becoming stale. Bodybuilders have for years been given bromides like "no pain, no gain," "high reps for definition, low reps for mass," "incline presses for upper pec mass," and had no means by which to test whether or not these recommendations were truly effective. With the advent of the Power Factor (and later, the Power Index), it became possible to test the claim made for every exercise you perform. You then simply calculate the results, which you can even illustrate by graphs to immediately see the effectiveness of a particular exercise and/or workout. This newfound technology has proved the fallaciousness of cookie-cutter routines that prescribe predetermined numbers of sets, reps, and weights irrespective of the tremendous physical and physiological variation between individuals.

WHY SPECIALIZE?

The truth is that some people may never need to specialize. Many individuals will receive tremendous stimulation from the workout we outline in *Power Factor Training* and will build all the muscle mass their frames can support simply from that routine. However, others find they have body parts that just aren't responding to the stimulus of exercise the way they should be. And others simply can't get too much of a good thing and want to take their muscular development of muscle groups like chest and arms to levels far beyond what they presently enjoy. For these two groups, specialization is the answer.

The advantage of specialization is that such intense, focused training allows the trainee to maximally stimulate a lagging body part into new levels of growth—without running the risk of overtraining. *Power Factor Training* established that performing more than five exercises in any one training session (providing, of course, that each set is a maximal effort) will quickly lead to overtraining. With Power Factor specialization—performed properly, as outlined in this book—you will be able to target lagging body parts (in this case, chest and arms) while still being able to keep your overall sets performed per workout low enough to prevent overtraining.

Specialization is not geared toward balanced development but toward the specific development of key muscle groups. In addition, specialization provides the additional psychological/motivational spur required to dissipate the monotony that inevitably follows whenever you lock yourself into any one activity for a prolonged period of time. This is a very important factor, as boredom does not encourage motivation, and unless you are highly motivated you will not reap the benefits that you should from any form of high-intensity training, particularly Power Factor Training.

Specialization properly done will rid you of the scourge of becoming stale almost indefinitely. In an attempt to further understand the need for specialization in training, our focus in this book will be two of the bodybuilder's most popular body parts: chest and arms. We will examine scientifically which exercises allow for the highest work per unit of time and, hence, provide the greatest growth stimulation to the chest and arm muscles.

By following this program you will be concentrating all of your body's adaptive energy into chest and arm development. This is a program that you should follow only for brief periods of two months or so during the year. If you try to perform this specialized training at the same time that you are performing other strength-building routines, you will short-circuit the benefits. This is a concentrated routine specifically designed to boost chest and arm development at the fastest rate of which your body is capable.

2

Power Factor Training
Fundamentals

In the event that you have never heard of Power Factor Training before, you need a quick lesson in how it is designed to maximize the efficiency and efficacy of strength training. Those who have read about it before will also benefit from this review of some of the most vital principles.

WHAT IS A POWER FACTOR?

Before the advent of Power Factor training, your only means of gauging the value of your workouts was by feel alone. If you felt particularly tired at the end of a workout, you probably assumed it was more productive than your previous one. The truth is, however, that your muscular overload may have been much less than you perceived it to be owing to inadequate sleep the night before, having consumed the wrong foods, or some other factor. The fact that you ended up tired and sore was not because you subjected your muscles to a greater overload at all; in fact, your workout might have been a total waste of your time and effort.

There are two keys to stimulating muscle growth:

1. subjecting your muscles to an overload of *a great amount of work in a unit of time*
2. making that overload progressively greater from workout to workout

Now, suppose you bench-press 150 pounds 30 times in 2 minutes today. And that's all you can do; you can't complete 1 more rep. Then you come back to the gym next week and bench-press 150 pounds 30 times in 1.5 minutes and that's all you can do; you can't get 1 more rep. Both days you lifted 150 pounds for 30 repetitions. But guess what? When you do it in 1.5 minutes you are stronger. It's a law of physics: the only way to lift the same amount of weight in a shorter amount of time is with a stronger "engine." If your muscles (the engine) are capable of lifting at a higher rate, they must be stronger. With conventional weight training, however, the time it takes to perform the lifting is completely ignored. In this example, if you ignored time, you would enter the results of the two workouts in your logbook and promptly get discouraged that you were not making any progress.

The Power Factor is a measurement of the total amount of weight you lift divided by the time it takes to lift it. It's measured in pounds per minute. Ask the average person in a gym what he bench-presses, and his reply might be "I can bench 275." Ask a person who uses Power Factor Training the same question and the answer might be "I can bench 5,300 pounds per minute." Because of the laws of physics and the law of muscle fiber recruitment, the latter is a much more comprehensive measurement. Once you begin to think in pounds per minute, your training objectives and progress become crystal clear.

Using Power Factor Specialization in your chest and arm workouts will enable you to calculate a precise Power Factor and Power Index for each exercise you perform. You will also be able to calculate at each exercise session what workout you need to perform next time in order to meet your goals of increased size and strength. This means that every workout can pay off in gains, and if it doesn't, you'll know exactly where and why you fell short. This level of precision and isolation represents a revolution in strength training.

ANALYZING BY POWER FACTOR

The purpose of calculating a Power Factor for each exercise that you perform is to provide a precise numerical measurement of your

Once you have a numerical measurement of your muscular output, you can compare the overload and effectiveness of every workout you perform.

muscular output. Once you have a numerical representation of your output, you can compare the overload and effectiveness of every workout that you perform. For example, let's take another look at the workouts of those two champions from Chapter 1.

Keep in mind that in both of these workouts the trainee would have given everything he had to complete his routine. It's not a case of Champion #2's really going all out and #1's just taking it easy. All of these sets could have been done to total muscular failure. If these two guys measured by feel, they would both be about as fatigued. But with Power Factor Training, measuring by feel is obsolete.

The fact is that by using the correct combinations of weight and repetitions, Champion #2 generated 600 percent more intensity, which translates into more muscle-growth stimulation.

Champion #1's Chest Workout

Exercise	Sets	Reps	Weight	Total Weight
Bench presses	1st	15	135 lb.	2,025 lb.
	2nd	10	155 lb.	1,550 lb.
	3rd	8	175 lb.	1,440 lb.
	4th	3	200 lb.	600 lb.
Incline presses	1st	12	105 lb.	1,260 lb.
	2nd	10	135 lb.	1,350 lb.
	3rd	9	145 lb.	1,305 lb.
	4th	8	155 lb.	1,240 lb.
Dumbbell flys (2 × 45 lb.)	1st	12	90 lb.	1,080 lb.
	2nd	12	90 lb.	1,080 lb.
	3rd	12	90 lb.	1,080 lb.

Total Weight: 13,970 pounds (weight 3 reps 3 sets)
Total Time: 30 minutes
Power Factor: 466 lb./min. (total weight ÷ total time)

Champion #2's Chest Workout

Exercise	Sets	Reps	Weight	Total Weight
Bench presses	1st	30	155 lb.	4,650 lb.
	2nd	30	155 lb.	4,650 lb.
	3rd	30	155 lb.	4,650 lb.
	4th	30	155 lb.	4,650 lb.
	5th	30	155 lb.	4,650 lb.
	6th	30	155 lb.	4,650 lb.

Total Weight: 27,900 pounds
Total Time: 10 minutes
Power Factor: 2,790 lb./min.

YOUR "SWEET SPOT"

There is a relationship between the amount of weight that you put on the bar and the number of times you can lift it. It's obvious— if the weight is very light you can do many reps but it takes a long time. If the weight is very heavy you can do only a few reps and the lifting will be over very fast.

Here's an example. Using the bench press, suppose that you want to determine your muscular output at the two ends of this spectrum. First you select a very light weight, let's say 10 pounds, and you perform sets of 40 reps at a time. After the 25th set you are completely fatigued and cannot perform another rep. All this takes 45 minutes. So, you lifted 10 pounds a total of 1,000 times for a total weight of 10,000 pounds. Since it took 45 minutes to lift all that weight, your Power Factor is 222 pounds per minute. That is a low Power Factor; a small child can lift more than 222 pounds per minute.

Next, you test the other end of the spectrum by lifting the heaviest weight you possibly can. So, you put 300 pounds on the bar, and mustering all the strength you can, you perform 1 rep. You rest for a few seconds, then try to get another rep but you just

There is a direct relationship between the amount of weight that you put on the bar and the number of times you can lift it.

can't. Three hundred pounds is your one-rep maximum. This calculation is easy; 300 pounds in 1 minute is a Power Factor of 300 pounds per minute. It's also a very low Power Factor, a fraction of what you are capable of generating.

This example demonstrates a critically important element of strength training. If you lift too light a weight you cannot generate a high Power Factor; yet, at the same time, if you lift too heavy a weight you also cannot generate a high Power Factor. Somewhere in the middle lies your personal "sweet spot," where the perfect combination of weight, reps, and time yield your highest possible Power Factor. Finding that spot is the key to maximum efficient and productive workouts. By the way, it varies considerably between individuals. The two graphs (on page 17) illustrate the point. Subjects A and B each experiment to determine how the weight they are lifting affects the number of reps they can complete in a 2-minute period.

As you can see, Subject A generates his highest Power Factor when he has 140 pounds on the bar. At that weight he can get the best ratio of total weight lifted per unit of time. That is his "sweet spot." Understanding this concept is the most critical element of Power Factor Training. He can put more weight on the bar—in fact he can lift 300 pounds—but if he does, the total weight he

Weight on Bar (lb.)	SUBJECT A			SUBJECT B		
	Total Reps	Total Weight (lb.)	Power Factor (lb./min.)	Total Reps	Total Weight (lb.)	Power Factor (lb./min.)
40	120	4,800	2,400	120	4,800	2,400
60	108	6,480	3,240	111	6,660	3,330
80	96	7,680	3,840	102	8,160	4,080
100	84	8,400	4,200	93	9,300	4,650
120	72	8,640	4,320	84	10,080	5,040
140	63	8,820	4,410	80	11,200	5,600
160	54	8,640	4,320	76	12,160	6,080
180	45	8,100	4,050	72	12,960	6,480
200	36	7,200	3,600	68	13,600	6,800
220	29	6,380	3,190	64	14,080	7,040
240	22	5,280	2,640	50	12,000	6,000
260	15	3,900	1,950	36	9,360	4,680
280	8	2,240	1,120	16	4,480	2,240
300	2	600	300	4	1,200	600

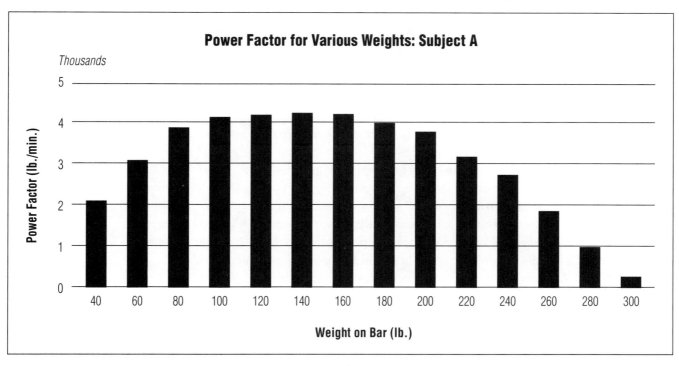

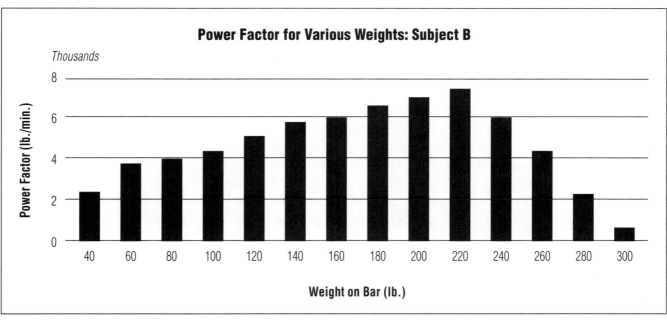

can lift per minute is greatly decreased. Since human muscles will grow stronger and larger only when they are taxed beyond their normal operating capacity, it is crucial to discover what your operating capacity is in the first place. Subject A can lift 280 pounds 8 times in 2 minutes and it will take everything he has to perform those reps, but it is nowhere near his muscles' full capacity for lifting. Therefore, while it might generate some adaptive response, it is very inefficient compared to his lifting 140 pounds 63 times in the same 2-minute period. This is a well-settled principle of physics. An engine that lifts 4,410 pounds per minute has to be more powerful than an engine that lifts 1,120 pounds per minute. Your muscle fibers are the engine; nothing else does the lifting.

Subject B demonstrates how variation occurs between individuals. His highest Power Factor is achieved when he has 220 pounds on the bar. He can put more or less weight on the bar, but his personal "sweet spot" is at 220 pounds. Why? There are many factors that contribute to the ability of muscle fibers to activate and to the power they generate. Some of the factors we know and some of them we are yet to fully understand. Where the muscle physically attaches to the bone relative to the joint has a profound effect on leverage. The neural pathways between the brain and muscles have varying efficiencies in individuals. The body's ability to supply and process adenosine triphosphate (ATP) to the muscles varies between individuals as do the mix of slow-twitch and fast-twitch fibers in each muscle, and the complex cocktail of blood, oxygen, amino acids, and hormones that supply the entire process has nearly infinite possibilities of variation. But here is the good news: all you have to concentrate on is developing your highest possible Power Factor for each exercise because it gives a clear indication of what is delivering the most overload to your muscles and what is not.

Now, of course you can't take blood samples and tissue biopsies after each exercise that you perform in order to analyze which technique is generating the greatest metabolic changes. And you certainly can't place your body in an MRI machine during each exercise to see what area of a muscle is activated by a particular exercise. And you can't perform a CAT scan on your brain to determine what neural pathways are being activated by today's workout. But you don't need to! If your Power Factor is 6,500 pounds per minute this workout and last workout it was 5,600 pounds, per minute, then you are absolutely, positively generating more output from your muscles. And who cares if it's because of hormone secretion or neural pathways or both? All these systems work together anyway, so isolating one or the other through complex testing does not really provide any practical benefit to the athlete who just wants results. Train by the numbers and everything else will take care of itself.

BETA STRENGTH AND THE POWER INDEX

The human body is a wonder of engineering. It has a remarkable variety of automatic survival and protection mechanisms that we are only beginning to understand. Breathe in some bacteria and one mechanism goes to work, cut your hand and a different mechanism kicks in. Jump into cold water or get under the hot sun and your body immediately goes to work compensating for the stress and sending survival signals to your brain. One of those safety systems prevents you from working out too strenuously. Call it fatigue, muscular failure, or running out of gas, it's what protects you from exercising to the point of putting too much stress on your body's recuperative abilities.

If you think of lifting weight as performing work the way a machine does, then there are two measures of that machine's strength or power. First there is the rate of lifting that it can achieve, like twenty tons per hour. Then there is the amount of time that the machine can sustain that rate of work, like four hours or twenty-four hours, before needing to be shut down. Your body has the same two forms of power, but there are protection mechanisms that try to prevent you from operating at their extreme limits. That's why you can perform a set to failure, but after only a few seconds' rest you can perform more reps with the same weight. Some people, after only 60 to 90 seconds of rest, can

exactly duplicate the first set to failure. That means that they have much more strength capacity but that it is not all tapped into in only 1 set. This phenomenon of hitting an initial wall of fatigue that can be overcome with brief rest is just one more protection mechanism of your body. It keeps extra muscular energy in reserve just in case it's required in the near future, like in 1 or 2 minutes, for example. If you never use that reserve amount of strength, it will never grow to a higher level because it doesn't have to.

We call these two forms of human power *alpha strength* and *beta strength*. Alpha strength is akin to a snapshot in that it gives a measurement of your rate of lifting for a moment in time, perhaps 1 minute or 2. Beta strength is more like a motion picture that can measure how long you can sustain your alpha strength. There is a subtle but extremely important difference. To illustrate the point, consider that the 1995 edition of the *Guinness Book of Records* lists John "Jack" Atherton as setting a record by bench-pressing 1,134,828 total pounds in twenty-four hours. That's a rate of lifting of 788 pounds per minute, a rate nearly anyone reading this could duplicate, but he sustained that rate for twelve hours! I can already hear some of you saying, "Twenty-four hours? That's aerobic exercise!" However, while there is no question that sustaining activity for that long is aerobic in nature, it was his muscles that lifted that million-plus pounds, not his well-developed heart and lungs.

On the other hand, the Bill Kazmaiers and Anthony Clarks of the world can generate the highest alpha strength. A 700-pound-plus bench press or a 900-pound-plus squat represents an astronomically high rate of instantaneous muscular output, which the human body will sustain for only a very short period of time. Here is the most important fact for bodybuilders in all of this analysis: both forms of strength build muscle mass. Mass is the ingredient that every bodybuilder is after, but how many realize that if they are not making progress with one method of strength building they can try another? Most bodybuilders don't really care about strength per se, they just want to increase it as a means to gaining more mass. But understanding how strength manifests in the human body can help you measure and guarantee your progress.

If strength can be increased in two ways, then we need to measure it in two ways. We measure alpha strength with the formula W/t, or total weight (W) ÷ total time (t) and beta strength with the formula $W^2/t \times 10^{-6}$, or total weight (W) squared divided by total time (t) divided by 1,000,000. These two measurements are the Power Factor and Power Index, respectively.

The Power Factor measures the intensity of your lifting (for example, a bench-press rate of 2,500 pounds per minute). In contrast, the Power Index is a relative measurement of how long you can sustain a given rate of lifting. Sustain 2,500 pounds per minute for 3.5 minutes and your Power Index is 21.9; sustain it for 11 minutes and your Power Index is 68.8. Please notice that in both cases your Power Factor is the same 2,500 pounds per minute; there is no difference in alpha strength.

In a strict sense, any discussion of how strong or powerful a person is depends on the period of time over which we are measuring. Over a 10-second period, Anthony Clark is king. Over 24 hours it's the aforementioned Jack Atherton. I wonder which of the two would be stronger over a 2-hour period? We frequently talk to frustrated bodybuilders who are making no progress because they have fallen into the trap of performing only 1 set, 3 sets, 30 reps, or whatever. What they don't realize is that they are always measuring their progress on a fixed, usually short, time scale. In effect, they measure progress by alpha strength only and never really tax that reserve sustained strength, their beta strength. All of them could make new progress by measuring their beta strength and then making sure that it progressively increases from workout to workout.

TWO WAYS TO GROW

There are two ways that you can get stronger. If you lift 2,000 pounds per minute today and last workout you lifted only 1,700 pounds per minute, then you are stronger. However, if you lifted 1,700 pounds per minute for 5 minutes last workout and this workout you lifted 1,700 pounds per minute for 7 minutes, you are also stronger, even though your Power Factor did not change. Why? Physics again. If an engine (your muscles) can continue lifting at a certain rate but for a longer period of time, it has to be stronger. You can't get something for nothing; more work done requires more strength.

As your Power Factor chest and arm training progresses, you will become familiar with the two ways to achieve higher Power Factors. Basically, you can either lift more total weight or you can lift the same weight in a shorter period of time. While both achievements represent an increase in muscular output, the tactic of constantly trying to work out in less time has obvious limitations. For one thing, the quicker your workout pace, the greater the likelihood of injury. Also, constantly reducing the time of your workout will lead to the ridiculous, a one-second workout per exercise. That won't tax your muscle's ability to generate its maximum power. Remember, being able to lift at the same rate but for a longer period of time is also an indication of increased strength.

As your chest and arm training progresses, you will become familiar with the two ways to increase your Power Factor numbers.

Note that you can achieve an extremely high Power Factor by performing certain exercises over a very short period of time. For example, suppose that you perform 6 wrist curls with 50 pounds in 6 seconds. Your Power Factor, based on a pounds-per-minute average, would be an impressive 3,000 pounds per minute! Of course, you really didn't lift 3,000 pounds, nor did you work out for 1 full minute, but your rate of lifting for $\frac{1}{10}$th of a minute would be 3,000 pounds per minute! This is the limitation of looking at Power Factor numbers in isolation. Theoretically, you could increase your Power Factor every workout by using the above tactic, but you'd be cheating yourself. This is where the Power Index measurement comes into play.

The Power Index is a mathematical function of the total weight lifted and the Power Factor. It simultaneously reflects both the total weight you lift and the rate of your lifting. Since the Power Index is calculated by multiplying the total weight by the Power Factor, the weight component of your workout is actually squared. This produces a very large number that is then divided by 1 million in order to make it more manageable. Using the example above of 6 50-pound wrist curls in 6 seconds (3,000 Power Factor), the Power Index would be only 0.9 (that is, 300 lb. $\times$ 3,000 lb./min. $\div$ 1,000,000). By way of contrast, we were routinely achieving Power Indexes in wrist curls of well over 30! Because it involves squaring the total weight lifted, the Power Index is graphed on a logarithmic scale. Consequently, the increases can be disproportionate both in raw numbers and in percentages (in fact, you shouldn't use percentages); a modest increase in strength can yield a large increase in the Power Index. The only important element is that the trend be in an upward direction. That is an indication of improvement and enough to guide you in the direction of progress. You can't cheat the Power Index. The only way to make big gains in your Power Index is to work toward lifting at a high Power Factor and to keep it up for as long as you can. In short, you must maintain a high muscular output (pounds per minute ratio) for as long as possible. The Power Index gives you a clear indication of whether or not your strength is increasing by measuring your capacity to continue lifting at the same rate but for a longer time. The Power Factor gives you a clear indication of whether or not your strength is increasing by measuring your capacity to lift at a higher rate.

Those are the only two ways your muscles (or any engine) can get stronger. By monitoring these two numbers, you will have instant feedback as to what exercises and techniques yield results and which do not. You can also instantly spot overtraining or a plateau. The efficiency of this system is what makes it revolutionary. As you will see, the gains you stand to make from doing so will be spectacular.

SISCO'S LAWS OF BODYBUILDING

A full understanding of the interrelationship between these various elements led to the development of Sisco's Laws of Bodybuilding. If you understand these principles, your training will take on a razor-sharp focus and you will also be immune to the crap that gets passed off as good training methodology.

1. Momentary intensity: $I_m = W/t$, where W is the total weight lifted in pounds and t is the total time in minutes. We express momentary intensity as a Power Factor (PF) in pounds per minute (for example, $PF = 2{,}150$ lb./min.). This measures alpha strength.

Since a high intensity of muscular overload is one of the indispensable conditions of triggering muscle growth, in the interest of greater precision and a more exact science, it behooves us to have a means of quantifying that intensity. In the realm of human exertion there are actually two forms of strength, which we (the authors) refer to as alpha strength and beta strength.

When we measure intensity with the Power Factor measurement we can identify and increase alpha strength. For example, if a trainee performs 20 reps with 200 pounds in 2 minutes, he has lifted a total weight of 4,000 pounds for a Power Factor of 2,000 pounds per minute (20 × 200 lb. ÷ 2 min. = 2,000 lb./min.). However, if next time in the gym that same trainee performs 20 reps with 200 pounds in only 1.5 minutes, his Power Factor increases to 2,666 pounds per minute (20 × 200 lb. ÷ 1.5 min. = 2,666 lb./min.). This increase in Power Factor accurately reflects the trainee's ability to perform the exercise at a higher intensity. Note that without this measurement on both workout days the trainee would simply enter "20 reps at 200 pounds" or "2 sets of 10 reps at 200 pounds" in his logbook and promptly get discouraged that he made no progress when, in fact, he made great progress.

2. The momentary intensity (I_m) of any exercise is inversely proportionate to the duration (D) that it can be sustained. This law is self-evident. The number of reps you can perform (and the time it takes to perform them) with 10 pounds is always more than with 100 pounds. Therefore the longer duration an exercise or workout is, the lower the momentary intensity must be.

3. Volumetric intensity: $I_v = W^2/t \times 10^{-6}$, where W is the total weight lifted in pounds and t is the total time in minutes. We

It is a fact of human physiology that the more intense the muscular output is, the shorter the duration for which it can be sustained.

express volumetric intensity as a Power Index (P_i) (for example, $P_i = 85.6$). This measures beta strength.

When we measure intensity with the Power Index, we can identify an increase in beta strength. For example, suppose a trainee performs an exercise with a Power Factor of 1,500 pounds per minute (his momentary intensity), and he is able to sustain that rate of lifting for 3 minutes before he is at failure. Then next time in the gym he still has a Power Factor of 1,500 pounds per minute, but he is able to sustain it for 4.5 minutes before he reaches failure. If we look only at his Power Factor measurement of momentary intensity he has made no progress. However, it is obvious that he is stronger, since he can sustain the same high level of muscular output for a longer period of time. This ability is his beta strength, and it is measured with the Power Index. His initial Power Index would have been 6.8, and his second Power Index would have been 10.1. This increase in Power Index accurately reflects the trainee's ability to sustain the intensity for a long period of time.

4. Frequency of training: $(F) = {}^R/_{I_v}$, where R is the trainee's recovery capacity and I_v is the volumetric intensity of the workout. The volumetric intensity (I_v) of a workout is inversely proportional to the frequency of training (F). This is due to the trainee's finite recovery capacity (R).

Human physiology is such that while a person can increase his muscular strength by a factor of at least 300 percent, his other supporting organs will not increase their functional capacity to the same degree. For example, there is a limit on how much cellular waste your kidneys can process in, say, a twenty-four-hour period. If you triple your strength through weight lifting, your kidneys will not also triple their efficiency or size so they can process more in twenty-four hours. Since organs like the kidneys, liver, and pancreas have relatively fixed rates of performing their functions and will not grow enormously larger and more efficient with more use, it is necessary to simply give them more time to complete their jobs as you get stronger.

At this time we have no unit of measurement for recovery capacity (R), and it certainly would vary enormously between individuals. It would also vary in the same person from time to time. For example, when ill or getting over an illness you would have a greatly diminished recovery capacity. What is important to remember is the principle that, because of a relatively fixed and finite recovery capacity, your frequency of training (F) must decrease as your volumetric intensity (I_v) increases. This is the law that prevents consistent progress when using a fixed training schedule. In other words, if you always train three days per week, you will reach a point where your volumetric intensity cannot be progressively increased. Without progressive overload there can be no new growth stimulation. You must decrease training frequency if you want to increase intensity. Like gravity, it's the law.

INTENSITY VS. DURATION

It is a fact of human physiology that the more intense the muscular output, the shorter the duration for which it can be sustained. This is what is known as an inverse relationship. For duration to increase, intensity must decrease and vice versa. Muscles increase their strength, power, and size in response to intensity of muscular output. Intensity is the dominant factor by far. That is why a sprinter's leg muscles are always bigger and stronger than a marathoner's leg muscles. It logically follows that to exploit this characteristic of human physiology to the maximum, exercises designed to increase strength should be as intense as possible. Duration actually becomes an excellent yardstick in this endeavor. By definition, the longer an exercise lasts, the lower its intensity.

Chapters 7 and 8 will show you routines that are designed to capitalize on this relationship and generate the most muscle stimulation possible.

RECOVERY

It has long been thought in bodybuilding that proper training tears down the muscle and then, if adequate recovery time has been allowed (typically twenty-four to forty-eight hours), the muscle will build up bigger than before. Unfortunately for those who

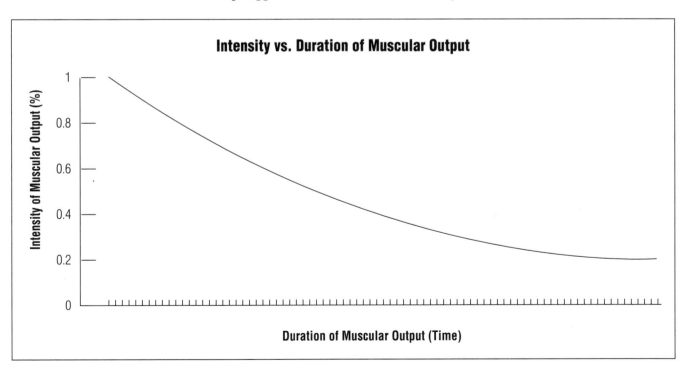

have made this principle the foundation of their training beliefs, it has proved itself false.

To begin with, proper training should never "tear down the muscle." A torn muscle is a damaged muscle, and that is injurious—never progressive. If you actually tore down your leg muscles when you went to the gym to train your legs, you would be unable to walk out of the gym after performing your first exercise.

What actually happens to a muscle during a properly performed workout is an alteration in muscle cell permeability, whereby certain enzymes leak through the cell membrane but there is no dramatic alteration in the structural integrity of the muscle as a result of working out. Productive bodybuilding training is engineered to stimulate the adaptive response of an increase in the strength and size of a particular muscle group—not cause cellular havoc. In other words, the workout sets into motion a series of physiological steps that culminate in the production of muscle growth—providing complete recovery and growth are allowed to take place.

All this leads us to the second fallacy within this belief, that any time off beyond twenty-four to ninety-six hours will lead to muscular decompensation or a loss of whatever strength and size gains were stimulated as a result of the workout. When we began research into Power Factor Training, there were three sources of supposedly valid training information: physiology textbooks, bodybuilding books written by authorities who were in some instances Ph.D.s (presumably in exercise science), and, as a last resort, the bodybuilding publications. In one and all, the attitude was that twenty-four to ninety-six hours was the maximum time a bodybuilder could afford to take off in between workouts if building and maintaining muscle mass was his goal.

Research presented in the textbook *The Physiology of Exercise for Physical Education and Athletics* (third edition) by Herbert A. de Vries of the University of Southern California, showed that "Workouts should be scheduled no less than three and no more than four times weekly for optimal results."[1] Ellington Darden, Ph.D., a popular bodybuilding and fitness author, makes the claim in his book *Strength Training Principles: How to Get the Most Out of Your Workouts*, that "Research has shown that there should be approximately forty-eight hours between workouts. In some cases, where extremely strong athletes are training, longer periods of time (seventy-two to ninety-six hours) are required. On the other hand, high levels of muscular size and strength start to decrease (atrophy) after about ninety-six hours of normal activity."[2]

In 1990, some thirteen years after writing the book from which the above quote was taken, Darden, then director of research for

Nautilus Sports/Medical Industries, simply repeated this "fact" in his book *New High-Intensity Bodybuilding for Massive Muscles Fast*: "Research has shown that there should be approximately forty-eight hours between high-intensity workouts. In some cases, where extremely strong athletes are training, seventy-two hours are required. On the other hand, high levels of muscular size and strength start to decrease after about ninety-six hours of normal activity."[3] He concludes "An every-other-day training schedule—Monday, Wednesday, and Friday or Tuesday, Thursday, and Saturday—is ideally suited for most bodybuilders."[4] After presumably another three years of research, Dr. Darden published his 1993 book *Grow: A 28-Day Crash Course for Getting Huge*, in which he again concluded, "With almost forty-eight hours of rest between two workouts and almost seventy-two hours after the third, a three-times-per-week exercise schedule allows for consistent growth stimulation and recovery overcompensation (i.e., muscle growth) within your major muscle groups. . . . A total body routine that is repeated three times per week is best for short-term and long-term growth."[5]

That same year, Matt Brzycki, a certified strength and conditioning specialist (accredited by the National Strength and Conditioning Association) and strength coach and health fitness coordinator of Princeton University, advanced a conclusion that embraced both falsehoods in his book, *A Practical Approach to Strength Training*:

> When you lift weights, your muscle tissue is broken down, and the recovery process allows the muscle time to rebuild itself. . . . A period of about 48–72 hours is necessary for muscle tissue to recover properly from a strength workout. Therefore, it is suggested that you lift three times per week on nonconsecutive days. Performing any more than three sessions a week gradually will become counterproductive. After about 96 hours without a resistance workout, the muscles begin to get progressively weaker.[6]

In 1996, three years after the publication of *Power Factor Training*, Mike Mentzer, a former Mr. Universe and articulate champion of the scientific method in bodybuilding, self-published a book titled *Heavy Duty II: Mind and Body*, in which he staked his claim as an authority on the fundamental principles of high-intensity training, including its corollary of recovery ability. After claiming "Presently, my understanding of the fundamental principles of the theory of high-intensity training is thorough and complete,"[7]

Mentzer went on to state that his research, born of personally training thousands of clients, has led to the conclusion that those seeking maximal increases in size and strength should "train once every ninety-six hours, or four days."[8] However, Mentzer stipulates that those who have been training for six to nine months can reduce their training frequency to "once every 6–7 days, or even less frequently."[9]

As science is an exacting discipline, the statement "even less frequently" is far from precise. In fact, it's downright vague for a man who has "thorough and complete" knowledge of the subject matter. However, the sad truth is that all of the aforementioned authorities are wrong. The break times they have advocated are entirely arbitrary and do not take into account the long-term depletion that attends productive exercise—nor have they factored in a method of assessing the innate adaptability variation that exists among individuals.

The facts are that rest requirements are directly related to a bodybuilder's existing level of strength and the amount of muscular output he has put forth in a given workout. Like most other human characteristics, the time required for complete recovery of the physical system to take place is highly individual. Two people may perform identical workouts and yet within twenty-four hours one may be fully recovered and overcompensated to the point that he would see an increase in his Power Factor numbers. The other individual might not reach this stage for another eight weeks. Hard to believe, you say?

Consider the following: The May 1993 issue of the *Journal of Physiology* reported that a group of men and women aged twenty-two to thirty-two took part in an exercise experiment in which they trained their forearms in a negative-only fashion to a point of muscular failure. Negatives are considered by some exercise physiologists to be more important than positive (concentric) contractions because more weight can be employed. In any event, all of the subjects agreed that they were most sore two days after exercising and that the soreness was gone by the ninth day. But it took most of the people nearly six weeks to regain just half of the strength they had before the workout! The study concluded that muscles are drained far more severely by intense exercise than was previously thought.[10]

According to this research, it can take months for the muscles of some individuals to heal and adapt after an intensive workout. This conclusion is corroborated by research that we have personally conducted with bodybuilders and golfers, in addition to our own personal experience. We once took a six-week layoff from training, and on our first day back in the gym set personal strength records on every exercise we performed. This further underscores the fact that there exist varying rates of recovery ability among individuals. The advantage of training by the numbers, by utilizing a Power Factor, is that you are able to precisely determine your personal range of recovery ability, which, depending on a variety of factors, may see you working out once every two days or once every four to five weeks.

Regardless of what your personal range of recovery happens to be, one thing is certain: everyone's personal recovery ability takes much longer to complete itself than many of the experts previously thought. To arbitrarily get your next workout in before ninety-six hours have elapsed is simply training scared—not training smart. But don't take our word for it; record your Power Factor and crunch your own numbers. You'll find when you come back to the gym, even if more than ninety-six hours have elapsed, that you won't be weaker at all.

The point is we're not asking you to take this on faith. There's a way to test and measure your recovery ability and the amount of time you should be taking in between your workouts. You can find out for yourself what is valid and what is not. They're called a Power Factor and a Power Index, and they consist of simple arithmetic—and there's no way we can trick you with mathematics.

FULL RANGE VS. STRONGEST RANGE

Let's suppose that most of what you've been told about not only recovery ability but weight training as well is wrong. Suppose that lifting weights through a full range of motion isn't the best way to build muscle mass. Let's seriously question this for a moment.

Where is it ordained, for example, that in order to stimulate maximum muscle growth a repetition must be performed through the greatest possible range of motion? In fact, where in the scientific literature has it—ever—been categorically established that a full range of motion is an absolute necessity if you seek to build superior levels of muscle size and strength? There are no answers to these questions because there simply is no evidence to support such conclusions. Nowhere at any time has it been established that lifting a weight through exaggerated ranges will result in anything but a mechanical disadvantage to both the joints of articulation and the muscle groups involved. In fact, there is evidence that such training practices are what lead to the bulk of injuries in bodybuilding, because it meant subjecting the joints and connective tissues of trainees to dangerously high sheer forces. Fortunately, there exists a better way to train. Since the introduction of Power Factor Training we have heard from countless people who have made the best gains in their bodybuilding careers by using strong-range partials only. They have also eliminated the frequent injuries that they used to experience. Many trainees have gained over thirty pounds of muscle in a few months performing brief, infrequent workouts that never, ever involved a full-range movement.

Utilizing conventional bodybuilding methodology, these gains would have been impossible. According to the conventional bodybuilding wisdom in such matters, muscle growth is a slow

Since the introduction of Power Factor Training, we have heard from countless people who have made the best gains of their bodybuilding careers by using strong-range partials.

process. The implication is that you must be patient, investing countless hours of sweat in your workouts every week, and then somehow, after hundreds of hours in the gym, you will be rewarded for your labors with a small amount of muscle gain and a nearly imperceptible difference in your physique. You'll be relieved to learn that this approach has no basis in scientific fact.

HOW MUSCLE TISSUE IS STIMULATED

The door to increased gains in muscle mass can be unlocked relatively easily—once you locate its key. And fortunately, the key is not hard to find: it can be found within the pages of any exercise physiology textbook. Furthermore, we'll save you the cost of buying one. Here's a snapshot of what science has revealed over the past century about how muscle tissue is stimulated to hypertrophy (that is, bigger and stronger).

THE BIRTH OF THE OVERLOAD PRINCIPLE

We've known that the persistent use of muscles causes their enlargement and a correlated increase in their strength ever since the early days of ancient Greek mythology, where Milo of Crotona was said to have gained great powers through his progressive lifting. The weight that Milo lifted onto his shoulders every day began as a calf. Naturally in time the calf matured into a bull, and with that maturity came great size, until it was a ponderous creature, too large for anyone but Milo to lift. However, the ancients said that the increments in the bull's weight came so gradually and progressively that Milo was able to build his strength accordingly and become a perennial champion of the early Olympic Games.

Whether or not this story is true, the principle that it relates certainly is. In many respects, Milo was probably our first exercise scientist. However, it wasn't until the research of the twentieth century that we have been able to understand the nature and limitations of this principle, along with the kind of exercise that brings it about and the laws that govern its development.

In 1905 an exercise physiologist by the name of W. Roux observed that the muscles of various athletes differed and that not all muscles in one athlete were equally large. He postulated that the size and strength of muscles were related not to the total amount of work done but rather to the amount of work done in a unit of time, that is, to the intensity factor.[11]

Approximately twelve years later, a student of Roux's by the name of H. Lange put a sharper point on Roux's research into hypertrophy in a little book that Roux himself published after Lange's passing. In his book, Lange says the following about hypertrophy:

> Only when a muscle performs with greatest power,
> i.e., through the overcoming of a greater resistance
> in a unit of time than before, would its functional

cross section need to increase. . . . If, however, the muscle performance is increased merely by working against the same resistance as before for a longer time, no increase in its contractile substance is necessary. . . . Hypertrophy is seen only in muscles that must perform a great amount of work in a unit of time. The athlete who in a few seconds generates great power in lifting a weight, in a fast run, or in a jump possesses massive musculature. Distance runners, walkers or swimmers lack the same.[12]

A classic demonstration of this principle produced by H. Petow and W. W. Siebert in 1925 helped to further establish this principle, throwing additional light on the nature and cause of muscle growth. The physiologists discovered that an increase in the gastrocnemius weight of rats was a function of the speed of running rather than of its duration.

The rats were exercised for a half year in motor-driven exercise wheels. All ran the same distance but at various speeds. Muscle growth was found in the leg muscles of the rats that were made to run at higher speeds. The physiologists also found that at a moderate speed, just enough to produce slight hypertrophy, conditions soon became stationary (i.e., muscle size didn't change) no matter how long the exercise continued and that further hypertrophy resulted only when the speed was markedly increased. Thus Petow and Siebert concluded that hypertrophy was a function of the amount of work performed in a given unit of time. Or, to quote the scientists directly: "Hypertrophy results from an increase in the intensity of work done (increase of work in a unit time), whereas the total amount of work done is without significance."[13]

Similar results were obtained more recently (1975) utilizing similar procedures when Dr. Alfred Goldberg and his colleagues at Harvard University made a rather profound discovery about muscle tissue. They observed that if adequate stimulation were present, muscle would grow—period. And it will grow in proportion to the severity or intensity of the stimulation. Further, they clinically established that muscle tissue would grow in the absence of insulin, testosterone, growth hormone, rest, and even food.[14] It grows solely in proportion to the degree of stimulation it receives.

Obviously this is not to imply that such conditions of deprivation are desirable or facilitate an atmosphere conducive to optimum growth, but the fact remains that stimulation is the primary factor in the muscle-growth process. (This explains the complete lack of muscle growth experienced by individuals who consume large doses of anabolic steroids but don't train.)

It follows from this that the greater the stimulation, the quicker the adaptive response of muscle growth. The question that now surfaces is, what constitutes *stimulation* for purposes of inducing such muscle growth? In a word, stimulation of a muscle tissue is accomplished via exercise. And virtually any type of exercise will impart some degree of stimulation to the muscles. In the case of the Harvard study cited above, the stimulation was provided to the plantaris and soleus muscles of laboratory rats by having them exercise on an exercise wheel. The faster or more intensely the rats ran on that wheel, the greater the hypertrophy, or muscle growth, that occurred.

By increasing the effective work output in a unit of time that the muscles of the rats were made to encounter, the researchers had provided sufficient stimulation to cause an adaptive response in the rats' muscles. This stimulus was expressed in the meters per minute (MPM) of the exercise wheel. In moving from the rodent to the primate world, we see a parallel in the muscular development of athletes who perform more work in a given unit of time, which is why in track and field, sprinters always have larger, more muscular legs than distance runners or marathoners.

The work performed in a unit of time by the sprinter (typically measured or expressed in miles per hour, or MPH, as opposed to the MPM of the rats' exercise wheel) is always greater than that done by the distance runner. Both types of athlete can cover a given distance, but the sprinter does it far more quickly.

Proper bodybuilding training, then, can be likened to that of the sprinter. The work performed in a given unit of time should be high—of the highest possible order if maximum muscle stimulation is desired—which means that the exercise performance should be fast and as heavy as possible (the effective workload).

A sprinter carries his or her bodyweight over a distance of, say, a hundred yards in as short a time as he or she possibly can. Likewise, the bodybuilder seeking to improve his or her muscular mass is not running but is nevertheless involved in moving a given weight a given distance as quickly as possible (increased work in a unit of time). The advantage the bodybuilder enjoys is that he is not limited to a fixed amount of weight (or work) that he must move in that unit of time. The sprinter moves only his or her bodyweight, whereas the bodybuilder can increase his training poundage, the effective intensity or workload, at will.

Intensity, the stimulus for muscle growth, is then a function of power input: you are moving weight a certain distance in a certain amount of time. So if you can increase the weight, increase the repetitions performed, and decrease the time it takes to do both, you will be increasing your power input and hence the stimulation for muscle growth geometrically.

Once increased work in a unit of time is isolated as the sole stimulus that induces muscular hypertrophy, it logically follows that an exercise that produces the greatest output or work in a unit of time will be the one that stimulates the greatest muscle growth. It was this unambiguous conclusion that led one of the authors of this book, Peter Sisco, to formulate a method to calculate the work per unit time, the Power Factor, of any given exercise.

ENTER THE POWER FACTOR

Once the Power Factor was formulated, we had in our possession a most effective tool by which to gauge the productiveness of any exercise and workout we performed. As one of the authors, John Little, is something of an exercise historian, he suggested that we experiment with a technique popularly referred to as *partials*. John had learned of this technique's effectiveness from conversations he'd had with bodybuilding legends Mike Mentzer, Lou Ferrigno, and Dorian Yates and from Olympic and powerlifting legends Bill Kazmaier, Anthony Clark, and the late Paul Anderson. We immediately discovered that partials, performed in the muscle's strongest range of motion, generated the highest possible work per unit of time and, hence, the highest level of muscle-growth stimulation.

The theory behind strong-range training is simple but enormously effective. Training in your strongest range allows you to utilize the heaviest possible weights, thereby applying the highest possible overload to your muscles to contract against for many repetitions. This results in an absolutely phenomenal rate of muscular output and, thus, growth stimulation.

Take the bench press as an example. The weakest range of motion in this exercise involves moving the weight the first few inches up from your chest. The strongest range of motion involves moving the weight the last few inches of your reach. As muscle fiber recruitment (and hence stimulation) is a matter of force requirements and not flexibility, the range of lifting is not a factor in the muscle-growth process.

In other words, if you can lift heavier weight, you will recruit more muscle fibers—regardless of the range through which you're actually lifting it. Further, the more repetitions you can perform with the heavier weight, the greater your work per unit of time and, as our scientist friends pointed out, the resulting hypertrophy.

To better illustrate this point, let us share with you an anecdote involving the authors' supervision of a recent champion bodybuilder's chest workout. This champion is exceptionally strong; the size of his muscles has to be seen to be fully appreciated. Further, his top repetition weight in performing full-range barbell incline presses is 315 pounds for 6 repetitions. This comes to a very respectable total weight lifted of 1,890 pounds (weight × reps = total weight).

Obviously, to move 1,890 pounds requires recruiting and stimulating a specific portion of muscle fibers. However, by utilizing a conventional or full range of motion, this champion was actually restricting his muscle fiber involvement. In fact, he was fully capable of handling much more weight in his strongest range of motion than he could in his weakest range (that is, full range). The former would have involved and stimulated even more muscle fibers into action and, hence, growth. How much more weight? Well, when we put him through a Power Factor Training workout, this champion performed strong-range incline presses with 605 pounds—for 12 repetitions! You read that correctly, and 605 pounds multiplied by 12 repetitions works out to a total weight lifted of 7,620 pounds from just that 1 set. Any way you slice it, lifting 605 pounds 12 times represents a far greater work-per-unit-of-time output than does lifting 315 pounds 6 times.

To continue with our illustration, at a later date we had our champion perform 4 sets of 6 reps on the incline press in full range with 315 pounds (for a total weight lifted of 7,560 pounds). Since

it took him 10 minutes to complete those 4 sets, his Power Factor (rate of lifting) was 756 pounds per minute (total weight ÷ total time). However, when we had him train in his strongest range of motion using partials, he increased the weight on the bar to 495 pounds (he'd performed 12 reps in this range with 605 pounds previously). In the same 10-minute time span, the champion was able to perform 4 sets of 20 strong-range partial reps with this resistance (for a total weight lifted of 39,600 pounds). His Power Factor in this scenario was a staggering 3,960 pounds per minute (total weight ÷ total time).

Switching to strong-range partials allowed him to substantially increase not only the weight his muscles were made to contract against but also his rate of work per unit of time (muscular output). This increase would have been impossible for him to obtain using conventional full-range exercise.

SPECIALIZATION VS. GENERALIZATION

One of the most important facets of bodybuilding is the fact that to engage in it successfully, three distinct phases must take place:

1. There must be an increased amount of muscular work in a given unit of time to induce new growth stimulation.
2. There must be time off to allow your muscles to recover from the workout.
3. There must be additional time off to allow your muscles to grow.

If you omit any one of these three phases, you will never realize any progress—despite your greatest efforts in the gym. If you attempt to train before you have fully recovered and overcompensated from your previous workout, all you will succeed in doing is prolonging the recovery process, as you will then have to recover from your present training session in addition to the prior one. And, if you allow enough time for recovery to take place but not enough time for growth to occur, you still won't grow. Why? Because it takes time for the growth process to be switched on, and no one is exempt from this basic law of biology—not you, your training partner, or Arnold Schwarzenegger.

It's not unlike the process of hair growth; that is to say, the growth of muscle tissue is a biological process that cannot be forced. You could go into a hair salon every day and have your hair professionally washed, styled, blow-dried, or cut—but that won't hasten the hair-growth process, which, being biological in nature, cannot be affected by anything other than your DNA. Your rate of muscle adaptation (innate adaptability to exercise) is also a genetically mediated process that occurs at a highly individual rate.

When we mention this process, we are referring to recovery of the physical system as a whole. Localized muscle recovery, as touched upon earlier, can take place quite rapidly in certain individuals, but that still doesn't alter the fact that the process of recovery always precedes that of the final growth process.

In fact, this last block of time is the most important requisite in the overcompensation, or muscle-growth, process apart from the initial strength stimulation itself. Of course, if you train with low intensity, you might well be able to recover sufficiently to train again the next day, but your progress in terms of gains in muscle mass will be minimal. And your objective as a bodybuilder should never be to see how much exercise you can withstand but rather to see just how little exercise is required to achieve the desired effect.

For example, let us assume that you have trained with sufficient muscular output to stimulate an increase in muscle mass; we'll call this phase 1. Phase 2 begins as soon as your workout has been completed. This is the stage of recovery. An individual muscle may, in some cases, recover fully within twenty-four hours or, in some extremely rare individuals, within even one hour. However, the recuperative subsystems that fuel your body and serve to mediate the recovery and growth processes require far more time to recover from the exhaustive and depleting effects of a growth-stimulating training session, and this amount will vary—in some cases quite widely—among individuals.

After identical workouts, for example, one bodybuilder may be able to return to the gym in forty-eight hours and note a strength improvement, while another bodybuilder may need as many as four weeks to go by in order to simply recover from his previous workout, and then another block of time on top of that to allow for the growth he stimulated in that one workout to manifest. Should he opt to train again—even though his muscles feel fine—before his subsystems have been fully replenished, then the only thing he will have accomplished will be diminished results. Recovery always precedes growth, and growth will not take place unless your muscles and the subsystems that feed them have completely recovered. It is crucial to never let your enthusiasm work against your objectives.

Phase 3, the phase in which the new muscle mass actually manifests, will take place only after complete systemic recovery has taken place. Exercise that results in a high muscular output in a given unit of time is a form of stress to the muscles and the overall physical system. When performed properly, such training will stimulate a compensatory buildup in the form of additional muscle strength that aids the body in coping more successfully with a stressor of like severity in the future.

The bodybuilders (at least those not on growth drugs) who insist on training six to seven days a week (whether on a system of three days on, one day off or four days on, one day off) will eventually witness a decompensatory effect, as the resulting drain on their regulatory subsystems will actually prevent the buildup of muscle strength. In fact, all of their energy reserves will be called upon simply to overcome the energy debt caused by such overtraining. However, if you train by the numbers, the gains will look after themselves and overtraining will become a thing of the past.

NOTES

1. de Vries, Herbert, A., *The Physiology of Exercise for Physical Education and Athletics* (third edition) (Dubuque, IA: Wm. C. Brown Company Publishers, College Division, 1980), 406.

2. Darden, Ellington, Ph.D., *Strength Training Principles: How to Get the Most Out of Your Workouts* (Winter Park, FL: Anna Winter Publishing, Inc., 1977), 37.

3. Darden, Ellington, Ph.D., *New High-Intensity Bodybuilding for Massive Muscles Fast* (New York: A Perigee Book, The Putnam Publishing Group, 1990).

4. Ibid.

5. Darden, Ellington, Ph.D., *Grow: A 28-Day Crash Course for Getting Huge* (Chicago: Contemporary Books, 1993), 97.

6. Brzycki, Matt, *A Practical Approach to Strength Training* (Indianapolis: Masters Press, 1993), 61.

7. Mentzer, Mike, *Heavy Duty II: Mind and Body* (Venice, CA: self-published by Mike Mentzer, 1996), 67.

8. Ibid., 104.

9. Ibid., 114.

10. *Journal of Physiology*, May 1993.

11. Steinhaus, Arthur, A., "Training for Strength in Sports," in *Toward an Understanding of Health and Physical Education* (Dubuque, IA: Wm. C. Brown Company Publishers, 1963).

12. Lange, H., *Über Funktionelle Anpassung USW* (Berlin: Julius Springer, 1917).

13. Petow, H., Siebert, W. W., *Studien über Arbeitshypertrophie des Muskels* (Z. Klin Medl, 1925), 102, 427–433.

14. Goldberg, Alfred, as reported in *Medicine and Science in Sports* (7:248–261, 1975).

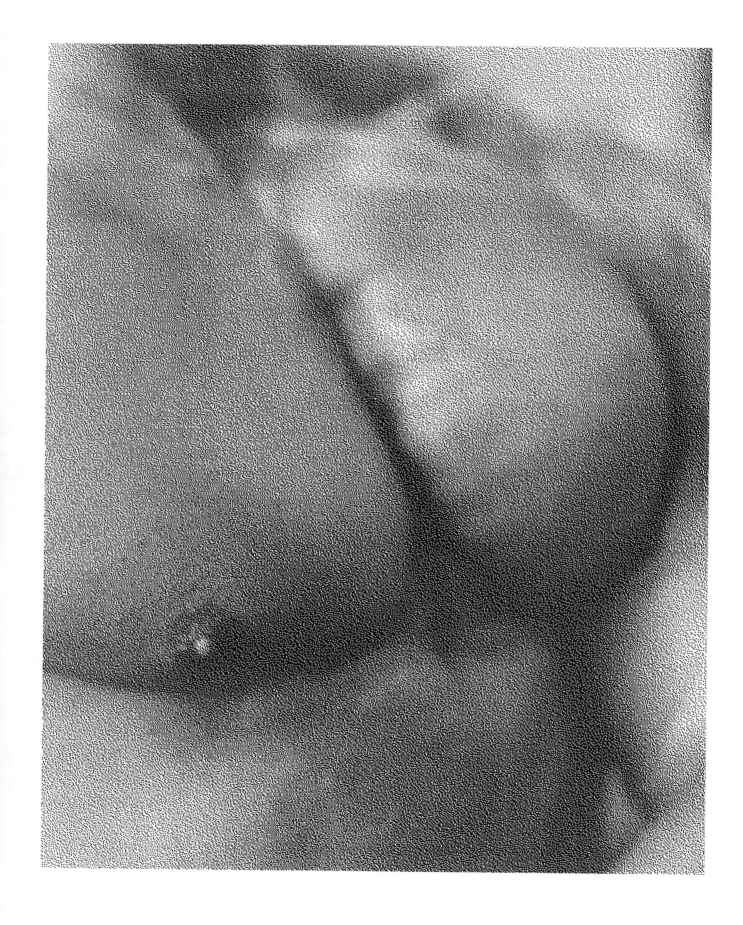

3

The Muscles of the Chest

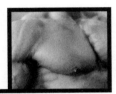

A well-developed chest on either sex is arguably the most admired body part. Women are concerned with ways to increase their "busts," and men, no differently, are concerned with increasing the size of their "pecs." This desire is particularly strong among teenage males who, in their unbridled desire to develop their chests so overtrain them (among other muscles) that growth, if it comes at all, proceeds at a snail's pace. Utter agony and frustration then ensue, and eventually the bodybuilder gives up in despair. This needn't be the case, however, if the pectoral-aspiring trainee employs the correct exercises and training principles.

How then should you properly perform your exercises? And just what exercises should you choose for the purpose of stimulating maximum growth in the pectoral muscles? And while we're at it, which exercise is truly the best for developing the chest? In this chapter we shall endeavor to answer these and other related questions.

THE CHEST—ANATOMY AND PHYSIOLOGY

There are, in effect, three different chest muscles; the pectoralis major, pectoralis minor, and serratus anterior, or serratus magnus.

Each of these must be fully stimulated as a result of your workouts if complete chest development is your goal.

The pectoralis major arises from the anterior surface of the sternal half of the clavicle, the anterior surface of the sternum, the cartilages of the true ribs, and the aponeurosis of the external oblique. *True ribs* refers to the anterior extremities of each of the first seven pairs of ribs that are connected with the sternum in front by means of the costal cartilages.

The fibers of the pectoralis major converge and form a thick mass, which is inserted by a flat tendon into the crest of the greater tubercle of the humerus, or upper arm bone. The action of the pectoralis major is as follows: if the arm has been raised, the pectoralis major acts with the latissimus dorsi and the teres major to draw the arm down to the side of the chest. Acting alone it adducts and draws the arm across the chest, also rotating the arm inward.

The pectoralis minor is underneath and entirely covered by the pectoralis major. It arises from the upper margins and outer surfaces of the third, fourth, and fifth ribs near their cartilages and is inserted into the coracoid process of the scapula (the little bump of bone on your shoulder). The action of the pectoralis minor is to depress the point of the shoulder and to rotate the scapula downward. In forced inspiration the pectoral muscles help in drawing the ribs upward and expanding the chest.

The serratus anterior or serratus magnus arises from the outer surfaces and superior borders of the upper eight or nine ribs and from the intercostals between them. The fibers pass upward and backward and are inserted in various portions of the ventral surface of the scapula. The action of the serratus is to carry the scapula forward and to raise the vertebral border of the bone as in pushing. It also assists the trapezius in raising the acromion process and supporting weights on the shoulder. It also assists the deltoid in raising the arm.

Another muscle involved in training the chest is the subclavius, which arises from the junction of the first rib and its cartilage and inserts into a groove on the under surface of the clavicle. The primary action of the subclavius is to depress the shoulder; that is, it carries the shoulder downward and forward.

CHEST EXERCISES

Note: The directions for the exercises in this chapter are for performing them using the standard full range of motion technique. Power Factor measurements, which we will discuss in

Chapter 5, were taken using full ranges for the purpose of having "apples to apples" comparisons of the intensities of the various exercises as most trainees perform them. Using the more enlightened strong range technique, trainees are able to generate enormously larger Power Factors, particularly in the most productive of these exercises.

Straight-Arm Pullover

Focus   The pectorals, the latissimus dorsi (and other muscles of the upper back that impart rotational movement to the scapula), and the triceps.

Performance   Lie back down on a flat bench and take hold of a barbell. Hold the bar at straight-arms' length over the chest with a slight bend in the elbow. From this position, lower the arms overhead, keeping the elbows bent slightly (although it is called a straight-arm pullover, a slight bend will remove any chance of your doing ligament or tendon damage to the shoulder or elbow joints) until a full stretch is felt in the latissimus dorsi muscle of the back. Return the bar to the starting position over the chest. We recommend that you inhale as you lower the bar to the full stretch position and then exhale as you raise it over the chest. Repeat.

Straight-arm pullover—start position

Straight-arm pullover—finish position

Nautilus Machine Pullover

Focus   The serratus, pectorals, latissimus dorsi, and other upper back muscles that place rotational force on your scapula and rectus abdominus.

Performance   Adjust the height of the seat so that your shoulders are at the same level as the cams when you sit in the seat. Sit down on the seat and rest your back against the back support throughout the movement. Secure the lap belt. Place your feet against the pedal directly in front of you and push down on the

Nautilus machine pullover—start position

Nautilus machine pullover—finish position

pedal to bring the lever arm of the machine forward to a position
in front of your torso. Place your elbows against the pads attached
to the lever arm, and lightly rest your fingers on the crossbar of the
lever arm. Release foot pressure from the pedal to place full resistance on the lever arm. Allow your elbows to travel in a semicircular arc as far to the rear as is comfortably possible. Use the
strength of your torso muscles to push the pads forward and downward in a semicircular arc until the crossbar attached to the lever
arm contracts your abdomen. Return slowly to the starting position. Repeat.

Flat Bench Cable Crossover

Focus   The entire pectoral complex, as well as the anterior deltoids.

Performance   Lie back on a flat bench that has been placed between two floor pulleys. Grab hold of a handle in each hand, and draw your hands together at arm's length above your chest with palms facing each other. Pause briefly. With your elbows

Flat bench cable crossover—start position

slightly bent, lower your arms out to either side in a wide semi-circular arc until there is a mild stretch on your pectoral muscles. Repeat, drawing your arms back toward the center still maintaining the semicircular arc motion.

Flat bench cable crossover—finish position

Dumbbell Fly

Focus   The entire mass of the pectorals and the anterior and medial deltoids.

Performance   To begin, grab hold of two dumbbells and lie back down on a flat bench. Hold the dumbbells over your chest with your arms fully extended and your palms facing each other.

Dumbbell fly—start position

Slowly lower your elbows out to the sides while keeping a slight bend in your arms. Hold this stretched position briefly before raising the dumbbells back up to the finish position. Repeat.

Dumbbell fly—finish position

Incline Barbell Press

Focus   The pectoral muscles, the triceps, and anterior and medial deltoids.

Performance   A special incline bench is required for this exercise, ideally one with supports to hold the weight. Lie back down on the incline bench and take a shoulder-width grip on the barbell. Extend your arms fully, thereby lifting the barbell from its

Incline barbell press—start position

supports. Pause briefly in this fully extended position to ensure proper balance. Once you've got proper balance, slowly and deliberately lower the barbell to your upper chest. Pause briefly in this position and then press it back to the start position. Repeat.

Incline barbell press—finish position

Nautilus 10-Degree Chest Machine

Focus   The entire pectoral complex, serratus, and anterior and medial deltoids.

Performance   Lie on your back with your head higher than your hips. Place your arms under the roller pads. The pads should be in the crooks of your elbows. Move both arms upward in a semi-

Nautilus 10-degree chest machine—start position

circular arc until the roller pads touch above your chest. Pause briefly in this contracted position and then lower your arms back to the starting position. Repeat.

Nautilus 10-degree chest machine—finish position

Unilateral High Pulley Cable Crossover

Focus   The entire pectoral complex, serratus, and anterior deltoids.

Performance   Attach a loop handle to an overhead pulley. Grab hold of a handle that is attached to a high pulley with one hand; place your free hand on your hip. Bend forward at the waist (maintain this torso angle throughout the duration of the set),

Unilateral high pulley cable crossover—start position

allowing your arm to extend upward. Draw the handle down and in front of you, keeping the handle at arm's length. Allow the handle to cross the midline of your torso. Pause in this position briefly and then return to the starting position. Repeat. Then switch sides and repeat the procedure.

Unilateral high pulley cable crossover—finish position

Bilateral High Pulley Cable Crossover

Focus   The entire pectoral complex, serratus, and anterior deltoids.

Performance   Using two overhead pulleys, grasp a handle in each hand and bend forward, extending your arms down and in front of you. Continue drawing your hands toward one another until both hands extend slightly past the midline of your torso. Hold for a moment, and then let your arms be pulled back to the start position. Repeat.

Bilateral high pulley cable crossover—start position

Bilateral high pulley cable crossover—finish position

Decline Barbell Press

Focus   The entire pectoral complex, serratus, anterior and medial deltoids, and triceps.

Performance   To perform this exercise you will need a special bench that declines and that has roller pads for your feet to hook under for additional support. Remove the bar from the supports at arms' length and hold it above the chest until you achieve a feeling of control and balance. Then lower the barbell slowly and under control to the lower chest. Pause briefly. Repeat.

Decline barbell bench press—start position

Decline barbell bench press—finish position

Barbell Bench Press

Focus   The pectorals, anterior and medial deltoids, triceps, latissimus dorsi, and upper back muscles that impart rotational force to the scapula.

Performance   Lie back on a flat bench so that your shoulders are pressed on it firmly. Take a bar to arms' length with a fairly wide grip. Lower the bar to the chest, and then press it overhead to arms' length, ensuring that you keep it fairly high up over the chest

Barbell bench press—start position

and not too far toward the abdomen when you lower it. Take a deep breath as you lower the bar to the chest, and breathe out as you complete the press to arms' length. Repeat.

Barbell bench press—finish position

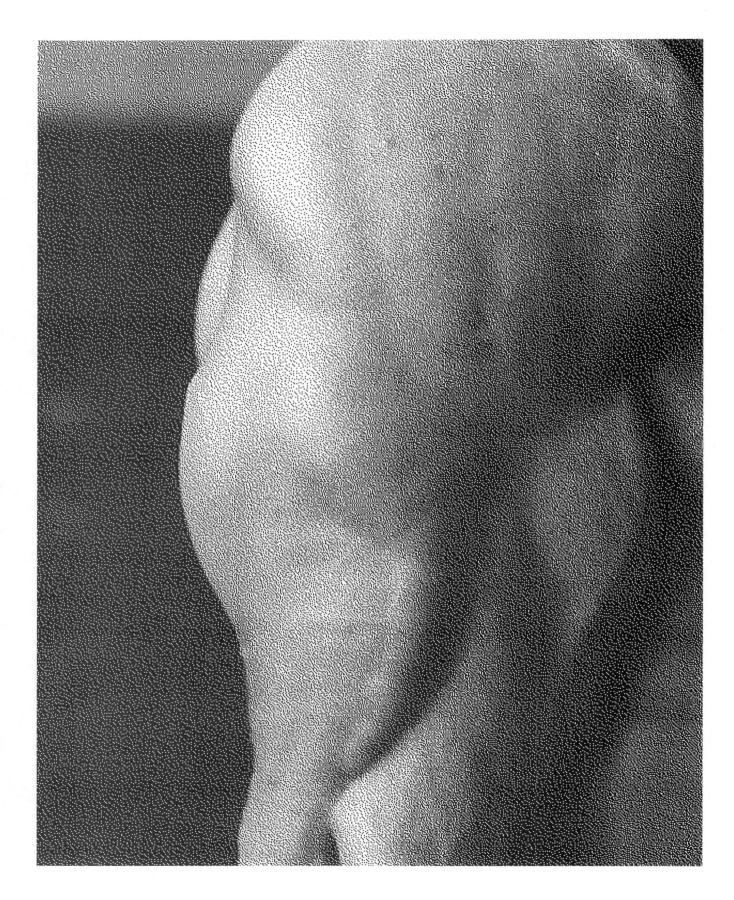

4

The Muscles of the Arms

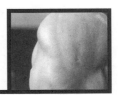

It's certainly not surprising that bulging biceps and massive triceps, replete with clearly delineated veins of garden hose dimensions, are the *sine qua non* of both the aspiring and competitive bodybuilder. The arms are without question the most enjoyable body part to train because they have a high pain threshold and are easy to pump up to fantastic proportions (a very important psychological spur in training). Whenever we're asked to make a muscle, it is always the arms that we flex in response.

As fun as the arms are to train, the old bromide about "too much of a good thing" is particularly true when you are caught up in the "pumpamania" mentality that most gym owners—and not a few bodybuilding magazines—tend to promote. It is very easy to overtrain your arms (or any other body part for that matter) and cause them to actually regress in terms of size and strength. This is why it is particularly important to pay attention to your Power Factor numbers when training the muscles of the arms.

Note: The directions for the exercises in this chapter are for performing them using the standard full range of motion technique. Power Factor measurements, which we will discuss in Chapter 6, were taken using full ranges for the purpose of having "apples to apples" comparisons of the intensities of the various exercises as most trainees perform them. Using the more enlightened strong range technique, trainees can generate enormously larger Power Factors, particularly in the most productive of these exercises.

THE TRICEPS— ANATOMY AND PHYSIOLOGY

The triceps, also known as triceps brachii, arises by three heads: the long head from the infraglenoid tuberosity of the scapula and the lateral and medial heads from the posterior surface of the body of the humerus, the lateral head above the medial. The muscle fibers terminate in two aponeurotic laminae, which unite above the elbow and are inserted into the olecranon of the ulna. The action of the triceps muscle is to extend the forearm, and its secondary function is to draw the arm down and past the midline of the body.

High pulley pressdown—start position

TRICEPS EXERCISES

High Pulley Pressdown

Focus The entire triceps complex.

Performance Take hold of a lat pulldown bar running through the high pulley of the machine (alternatively, you can use a handle in which the ends are angled downward, or one consisting of two parallel strands of rope). Take an overhand grip on the bar, your index fingers no more than 3 to 4 inches apart. Standing erect with your feet about 6 inches back from the pushdown station, bend your arms fully and press your upper arms against the sides of your torso.

Keeping your upper arms and body motionless, straighten your arms until your triceps muscles are fully contracted. Hold this position briefly and then return the bar back to the start position. Repeat.

High pulley pressdown—finish position

Lying Low Pulley Triceps Curl

Focus   The entire triceps muscle complex.

Performance   Attach a short bar handle to a low pulley. Taking hold of the bar, lie back down on a flat bench, your head at the end of the bench that is closest to the low pulley. Use triceps strength only to pull the bar handle upward so that your arms are locked out straight and angled directly upward, perpendicular to

Lying low pulley triceps curl—start position

the gym floor. To go back to start position, keep your upper arms motionless while bending your elbows to allow the pulley handle to descend in a semicircular arc behind your head. Continue until your arms are fully bent. Repeat.

Lying low pulley triceps curl—finish position

Nautilus Triceps Machine

Focus   The triceps muscles at the backs of the upper arms.

Performance   Adjust the height of the machine seat so your upper arm is parallel to the floor when resting on the pad. With your right hand facing your left at all times, place your right hand and wrist against the pads attached to the right-side lever arm of the machine. Use triceps strength to completely extend your right arm. Hold this peak-contracted position for a moment, and then allow the weight on the machine to pull your arm back to the start position. Repeat. Then switch sides and repeat the exercise.

Nautilus triceps machine—start position

Nautilus triceps machine—finish position

Bent-Over Dumbbell Triceps Extension (Triceps Kickback)

Focus   The entire triceps muscle complex.

Performance   Many people find the position required to perform the bent-over dumbbell extension a little uncomfortable. With one knee resting on a flat bench and one arm holding the bench to stabilize the body, grasp a dumbbell in your right hand. Maintaining the bent-over position with your free arm resting on the bench and your right arm locked perfectly straight, raise the dumbbell backward and upward as far as possible. Don't hold the finish position for any length of time, but you should try to make this a really fierce contraction (you will most certainly feel your triceps "burn"). Lower the dumbbell back to the start position. Repeat. Then switch hands and repeat the procedure.

Bent-over dumbbell triceps extension—start position

Bent-over dumbbell triceps extension—finish position

Standing One-Arm Dumbbell Triceps Extension
(Triceps Curl)

Focus   The entire triceps muscle complex.

Standing one-arm dumbbell triceps extension—start position

Performance   While standing, take hold of a dumbbell in one hand and hold it fully extended overhead. Keeping your elbow perfectly stable and close to your head, lower the dumbbell in a semicircular arc behind your head as far as you can. Then press the dumbbell back up to the start position. Repeat. Then switch hands and repeat the procedure to work the other arm.

Standing one-arm dumbbell triceps extension—finish position

Standing Barbell Triceps Extension

Focus   The entire triceps muscle complex.

Performance   A barbell is satisfactory for this exercise, which targets the triceps muscles in isolation. In a standing position, take hold of a barbell and raise it to arms' length overhead. Lower the barbell behind your head to the start position, keeping the elbows perfectly stationary. This is important: the elbows must remain

Standing barbell triceps extension—start position

pointing straight up; only the forearms move. Keeping the upper part of the arms as steady as possible, straighten the arms overhead once again, locking them fiercely at the completion of the movement. Make sure that you lower the bar to its original position behind the neck and resist the temptation to limit the extent of the lift. Repeat.

Standing barbell triceps extension—finish position

Seated Barbell Triceps Extension

Focus   The entire triceps muscle complex.

Performance   Perform this version of the previous exercise seated, so that your lower back is stabilized. Take hold of a barbell and raise it to arms' length overhead. Sit down on a flat bench and make sure the bar is perfectly balanced. From the overhead position, lower the barbell behind your head to the start position,

Seated barbell triceps extension—start position

keeping the elbows perfectly stationary. This is important: the elbows must remain pointing straight up; only the forearms move. Keeping the upper arms as steady as possible, straighten the arms overhead, locking them fiercely at the completion of the movement. Make sure that you lower the bar to its original position behind the neck and resist the temptation to limit the extent of the lift. Repeat.

Seated barbell triceps extension—finish position

Close-Grip Bench Press

Focus   The entire triceps complex, the pectorals, and the anterior and medial deltoids (in addition to the latissimus dorsi and the upper back muscles that impart rotational force to the scapula).

Performance   Lie back down on a flat bench so that your shoulders are pressed firmly against it. Take a close grip on the barbell, so that your hands are approximately a thumb's length apart, and press the barbell out to arms' length. Lower the barbell to your

Close-grip bench press—start position

chest, pause briefly, and then press it overhead to the start position once again. Repeat.

Close-grip bench press—finish position

Hammer Strength Dip Machine

Focus   The entire triceps complex, the pectorals, and the anterior and medial deltoids (in addition to the latissimus dorsi and the upper back muscles that impart rotational force to the scapula).

Performance   This is actually an excellent upper body developer, but the majority of focus is upon the triceps brachii of the upper arm. Position yourself in the seat so that your arms are just

Hammer Strength dip machine—start position

slightly behind your back when fully extended. This will ensure that the secondary function of the triceps, to draw the arm down and behind the midline of the body, is fulfilled. From a seated position with your arms fully locked out, holding onto the handles of the Hammer Strength dip machine, slowly break the lock in your arms and allow your hands to come to a point where they are almost in contact with your armpits. Repeat.

Hammer Strength dip machine—finish position

THE BICEPS—ANATOMY AND PHYSIOLOGY

The biceps, also known as biceps brachii, arises by two heads, hence its name. The long head arises from the tuberosity at the upper margin of the glenoid cavity, and the short head from the coracoid process in common with the coracobrachial muscle. Elongated bodies succeed these tendons, which are separate until within a short distance (seven centimeters) of the elbow joint, where they unite and terminate in a flat tendon, which is inserted into the tuberosity of the radius. The action of the biceps is flexion of the elbow and to a lesser extent of the shoulder, and the supination of the hand.

BICEPS EXERCISES

Standing low pulley curl—start position

Standing Low Pulley Curl

Focus   The biceps primarily and the brachialis and forearm flexors secondarily.

Performance   After attaching a bar to the end of a floor pulley, stand up straight and let your arms hang down at your sides. Set your feet about shoulder width apart, 1 to 1½ feet back from the pulley station. Press your upper arms against the sides of your torso and keep them motionless in this position for the duration of your entire set. You must also avoid moving your upper body as you perform this exercise. Using biceps strength only, curl the bar upward in a semicircular arc from the front of your thighs to a point beneath your chin. Lower the bar to the start position. Repeat.

Standing low pulley curl—finish position

Seated Scott Dumbbell Curl

Focus   The biceps primarily and the brachialis and forearm flexors secondarily.

Performance   Employ a Scott (preacher) bench for this exercise. Grasp a dumbbell in your right hand and place your left hand on the angled surface of the bench. The upper edge of the bench should be just under your armpit. From a position of full extension,

Seated Scott dumbbell curl—start position

slowly curl the weight up to your shoulder. Pause briefly and then lower the resistance back to the start position of full extension. Repeat. Then switch sides and repeat the procedure.

Seated Scott dumbbell curl—finish position

Lying Dumbbell Curl

Focus   Overall biceps and forearm flexors.

Performance   Grasp a pair of dumbbells and lie back down on a flat bench. Allow your arms to hang straight down from your shoulders. Using only the strength of your biceps muscles, curl the dumbbells simultaneously upward to shoulder level. Pause briefly in this position and then lower the dumbbells back to the start position. Repeat.

Lying dumbbell curl—start position

Lying dumbbell curl—finish position

Nautilus Machine Curl

Focus   The biceps and only minimal stress on your forearm flexor muscles.

Performance   Adjust the seat height so that your upper arms are parallel with the floor when resting on the pad. Rest your upper right arm on the pad, keeping it tucked against the small right-hand vertical pad throughout the movement. Grasp the handle attached to the lever arm of the machine with your right palm facing upward, and straighten your arm completely. Using the strength of your biceps muscle, curl the handle up to your right shoulder. Hold this position for a distinct pause, and then lower the handle back to the start position. Repeat. Then switch sides and repeat the process with your other arm.

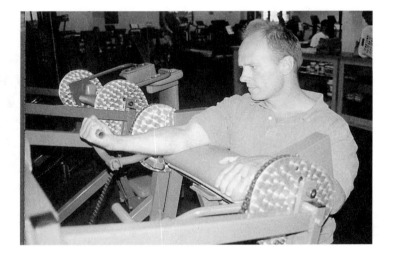

Nautilus machine curl—start position

Nautilus machine curl—finish position

Standing Scott Dumbbell Curl

Focus   The biceps and the flexor muscles of the forearms.

Performance   To perform this exercise you will need a special Scott (or preacher) bench that is freestanding. Grab hold of a dumbbell in your right hand and position yourself with your chest against the Scott bench and your right arm extending over its surface. Making sure to hold your body steady (you can grasp the top

Standing Scott dumbbell curl—start position

or edge of the angled surface of the bench with your free hand for stability), curl the dumbbell all the way up until it almost touches your chin. Pause briefly in this position and then lower it all the way back down to full extension. Repeat. Then switch sides and repeat the procedure for your other arm.

Standing Scott dumbbell curl—finish position

Seated Scott Barbell Curl

Focus The biceps and flexor muscles of the forearms.

Performance Taking an underhand grip on a barbell, sit down on a Scott bench with your arms extending over its surface. Lean slightly over the bench, making sure that your arms are running parallel to each other down the angled surface of the bench, your hands facing up at the lower end. The upper edge of the Scott

Seated Scott barbell curl—start position

bench should be just under your armpits, and your arms should be fully straightened. Using biceps strength only, curl the barbell up toward your chin. Pause briefly at the top and then lower the barbell back to the start position. Repeat.

Seated Scott barbell curl—finish position

Standing Scott Barbell Curl

Focus   The biceps and flexor muscles of the forearms.

Performance   To perform this exercise you will need a special Scott (or preacher) bench that is freestanding. Grab hold of a barbell and position yourself with your chest against the Scott bench and your arms extending over its surface. Making sure to hold your

Standing Scott barbell curl—start position

body steady, curl the barbell all the way up until it almost touches your forehead. Pause briefly in this position and then lower it all the way back down to full extension. Repeat.

Standing Scott barbell curl—finish position

Standing Dumbbell Curl

Focus   The biceps and the flexors of the forearms.

Performance   This exercise fulfills both the primary and secondary functions of the biceps: elbow flexion and supination. To begin, pick up two dumbbells and hold them at your sides, palms facing each other. Slowly curl the dumbbell in your right hand up toward your shoulder turning your palm outward (your arm should

Standing dumbbell curl—start position

be supinated as much as is physiologically possible). Pause briefly in this position and then lower the dumbbell back to the start position. Perform the movement with your left arm, and alternate in a seesaw fashion for as many repetitions per arm as you care to do.

Standing dumbbell curl—finish position

Seated Dumbbell Curl

Focus   The biceps and the flexors of the forearms.

Performance   To begin, pick up two dumbbells and sit down on a flat bench, allowing the dumbbells to hang straight down from your shoulders at your sides. From this start position, curl both

Seated dumbbell curl—start position

dumbbells up toward your shoulders. Pause briefly in this position and then lower the dumbbells back to the start position. Repeat.

Seated dumbbell curl—finish position

Hammer Strength Machine Biceps Curl

Focus   The biceps and minimal stress on your forearm flexor muscles.

Performance   Place the amount of weight you require on the peg on the curling machine. Next, adjust the seat height so that your arms rest on the pad parallel with the floor. Rest your upper arms on the pad, tucking them against the small vertical pads throughout the movement. Grasp the handles attached to the

Hammer Strength machine biceps curl—start position

lever arm of the machine with both hands and straighten your arms completely. Using the strength of your biceps muscles, curl the handles up to your chin. Hold this position for a distinct pause, and then lower the handles back to the start position. Repeat.

Hammer Strength machine biceps curl—finish position

Standing Barbell Curl

Focus   The biceps and the flexors of the forearms.

Performance   Grasp a barbell with a shoulder-width grip and palms facing forward. Stand upright with your arms hanging straight down and the backs of your hands next to your thighs. Maintaining this erect position, slowly curl the weight up to your

Standing barbell curl—start position

shoulders by bending your elbows, keeping your upper arms perfectly still. Bring the bar right up to your chin and flex hard, making sure to hold this maximum contraction briefly before lowering the barbell to the start position. Repeat.

Standing barbell curl—finish position

Seated Barbell Curls

Focus   The biceps and the flexors of the forearms.

Performance   To begin, pick up a barbell and sit down on a flat bench. Rest the barbell across your lap with your arms slightly bent. From this start position, curl the barbell up toward your

Seated barbell curl—start position

shoulders. Pause briefly and then lower the barbell back to the start position. Repeat.

Seated barbell curl—finish position

THE FOREARMS— ANATOMY AND PHYSIOLOGY

The forearm muscles are among the most impressive on the human body. The more you can isolate the forearms (that is, in the sense of limiting the influence of the upper arms) when you train them, the greater your muscular gains in the forearms will be.

The forearm muscles are called antibrachial and are divided into a volar (that is, pertaining to the palm) and a dorsal group. The volar group is further subdivided into a superficial and a deep group. The important muscles of the volar group and their functions are as follows:

Volar Superficial Group
- pronator teres—rotates the radius upon the ulna and renders the hand prone
- flexor carpi radialis—flexes and abducts the wrist
- palmaris longus—flexes the wrist joint and assists in flexing the elbow
- flexor carpi ulnaris—flexes and abducts the wrist and assists in bending the elbow
- flexor digitorum sublimus—flexes the middle and proximal phalanges and assists in flexing the wrist and elbow

Volar Deep Group
- flexor digitorum profundus—flexes the phalanges
- flexor pollicis longus—flexes the bones of the thumb
- pronator quadratus—rotates the radius upon the ulna

The volar forearm muscles arise from the medial epicondyle of the humerus and from the anterior surface of the radius and ulna near the elbow joint. They are inserted into the body of the radius, the carpals, metacarpals, phalanges, and the aponeurosis of the palm of the hand.

The dorsal group is also divided into a superficial and a deep group. The muscles of the dorsal group and their functions are as follows:

Dorsal Superficial Group
- brachioradialis—flexes the elbow joint and assists in bringing the hand into a supine position
- extensor carpi radialis longus—extends the wrist and abducts the hand
- extensor carpi radialis brevis—extends the wrist and abducts the hand

- extensor digitorum communis—extends the phalanges, then the wrist, and finally the elbow
- extensor digiti quinti proprius—extends the little finger
- extensor carpi ulnaris—extends the wrist
- anconeus—assists the triceps in extending the forearm

Dorsal Deep Group
- supinator—assists the biceps in bringing the hand into a supine position
- abductor pollicis longus—carries the thumb laterally from the palm of the hand
- extensor pollicis brevis—extends the proximal phalanx of the thumb
- extensor pollicis longus—extends the terminal phalanx of the thumb
- extensor indicis proprius—extends the index finger

The dorsal forearm muscles arise from the lateral epicondyle of the humerus and the posterior surface of the ulna and radius. They are inserted into the body of the radius, the metacarpals, and the phalanges. The action of the forearm muscles is to extend the elbow; extend, adduct, and abduct the wrist; extend the fingers; and supinate and pronate the hand.

The muscles of the hand are divided into three groups:

- The lateral volar (or thumb) muscles are located on the radial side and form the thenar eminence.
- The medial volar (or little finger) muscles are located on the ulnar side and form the hypothenar eminence.
- The intermediate muscles are located in the middle of the palm and between the metacarpal bones. These muscles act upon the thumb and fingers.

FOREARM EXERCISES

Seated Low Pulley Reverse Wrist Curl

Focus   The extensor muscles of the forearms.

Performance   Attach a bar handle to the end of a cable running through a low pulley. Take a shoulder-width overhand grip on the

Seated low pulley reverse wrist curl—start position

handle. Sit down on flat bench about 2 feet back from the pulley. Rest your forearms on your thighs, hands and wrists hanging off your knees. Gooseneck your wrists downward as far as you can. Using the strength of your forearm extensors, curl the handle upward in a small semicircular arc to a position in which your wrists are fully flexed. Lower the handle back to the start position. Repeat.

Seated low pulley reverse wrist curl—finish position

Seated Low Pulley Wrist Curl

Focus   The flexor muscles of the forearms.

Performance   Attach a bar handle to the end of a cable running through a low pulley. Take a shoulder-width underhand grip on the handle. Sit down on a flat bench about 2 feet back from the pulley. Rest your forearms on your thighs, hands and wrists hanging off your knees. Allow your wrists to extend downward as far

Seated low pulley wrist curl—start position

as you can. Using the strength of your forearm flexors only, curl the handle upward in a small semicircular arc to a position in which your wrists are fully flexed. Lower the handle back to the start position. Repeat.

Seated low pulley wrist curl—finish position

Standing Dumbbell Reverse Curl

Focus   The brachialis, the pronator teres, and the flexors of the forearms.

Performance   To begin, pick up two dumbbells and hold them at your sides with your palms facing toward each other. Curl both

Standing dumbbell reverse curl—start position

dumbbells up toward your shoulders. Pause briefly in this position and then lower the dumbbells back to the start position. Repeat.

Standing dumbbell reverse curl—finish position

Standing Barbell Reverse Curl

Focus   All variations of reverse curls place primary stress on the upper, outer forearm muscles, biceps, and brachialis muscles; secondary stress is on the forearm flexors, assisted by the pronator teres and quadratus.

Performance   To perform this movement, take an overhand grip on a barbell and stand erect with your arms hanging straight down from your shoulders. Press your upper arms against the sides of

Standing barbell reverse curl—start position

your torso in this position, and keep them motionless like this throughout your set, making sure to keep your wrists straight. Without allowing your torso to move forward or backward, slowly curl the barbell upward in a semicircular arc from the start position to a position directly beneath your chin. Tense your upper-arm and forearm muscles as tightly as possible in this position for a moment and then lower the bar back to the start position. Repeat.

Standing barbell reverse curl—finish position

Seated Barbell Reverse Wrist Curl

Focus   The upper, outer forearm muscles, biceps, and brachialis muscles; secondary stress is on the forearm flexors, assisted by the pronator teres and quadratus.

Performance   To perform this movement, take an overhand grip on a barbell and sit down on a flat bench, keeping your back perfectly straight. Rest the barbell on the tops of your thighs and slightly bend your elbows. Press your upper arms against the sides

Seated barbell reverse wrist curl—start position

of your torso in this position, and keep them motionless like this throughout your set, making sure to keep your wrists straight. Without allowing your torso to move forward or backward, slowly curl the barbell upward in a semicircular arc from the start position to a position directly beneath your chin. Tense your upperarm and forearm muscles as tightly as possible in this position for a moment and then lower the bar back to the start position. Repeat.

Seated barbell reverse wrist curl—finish position

Seated Dumbbell Reverse Wrist Curl

Focus   The extensor muscles of the forearm.

Performance   Take an overhand grip on a dumbbell so that your palm is facing the floor. Rest your free hand on your knee. Sit on a chair or stool with the forearm resting on your thigh so that your hand extends two or three inches in front of your knee. Maintain this position and gooseneck your wrist, lowering the dumbbell as

Seated dumbbell reverse wrist curl—start position

far as possible. Then, contracting only the extensor muscles of your forearm, raise the dumbbell by forearm strength only. Hold the fully contracted position momentarily and then lower the dumbbell back to the start position. Repeat. Then switch sides and repeat the procedure with your opposite forearm.

Seated dumbbell reverse wrist curl—finish position

Seated Barbell Wrist Curl

Focus   The flexor muscles on the underside of the forearm.

Performance   To begin this exercise, grasp a barbell with your palms facing upward and your hands spaced shoulder width apart. Sit down on a flat bench and rest your forearms on the tops of your thighs so that your hands extend 2 to 3 inches in front of your

Seated barbell wrist curl—start position

knees. Lower your wrists as far as possible and then contract the flexor muscles of your forearms, raising the barbell by forearm strength only. Return to the start position and repeat. Grasp the barbell tightly; only the hands move in this exercise.

Seated barbell wrist curl—finish position

Seated Dumbbell Wrist Curl

Focus   The flexor muscles of the forearm.

Performance   Take an underhand grip on a dumbbell so that your palm faces the ceiling. Your free hand can rest on your knee. Sit on a chair or stool with the back of the forearm holding the dumbbell resting on your thigh so that the hand extends 2 or 3 inches in front of your knee. Maintain this position and lower the dumbbell as far as possible. Then, contracting only the flexor muscles of your forearm, raise the dumbbell by forearm strength only. Hold the fully contracted position momentarily and then lower the dumbbell back to the start position. Repeat. Then switch hands and repeat the procedure for your opposite forearm.

Seated dumbbell wrist curl—start position

Seated dumbbell wrist curl—finish position

Standing Barbell Wrist Curl Behind Back

Focus   The flexor muscles of the forearm.

Performance   Place a barbell crosswise on a high, flat bench. Back up to the bench and grip the bar with your hands set 3 to 4 inches wider than your shoulders on either side. Stand erect with your arms hanging straight down from your shoulders and the bar resting across the backs of your upper thighs. Contract the flexor muscles of your forearms, raising the barbell by forearm strength only. Pause briefly in the fully flexed position and then lower the barbell to the start position. Repeat. Grasp the barbell tightly; only the hands move in this exercise.

Standing barbell wrist curl behind back—start position

Standing barbell wrist curl behind back—finish position

5

Rating the Chest Exercises

WHAT ARE WE TRYING TO PROVE THIS TIME?

Our readers have come to expect certain things from us in the realm of exercise science. Each of our books has revealed some new information that has enabled bodybuilders, strength athletes, and even casual exercisers to improve their performance enormously.

Power Factor Training introduced the concept of the Power Factor and Power Index as a means to measure the muscular intensity of exercise. Using those measurements that book went on to prove the enormous benefits of exercising in only the strongest range of motion by using weights that were much heavier than can be handled in full-range exercises.

Static Contraction Training went on to prove that the range of motion could be reduced even to zero and still there would be enormous gains in muscle size and strength. That book also proved that the new strength transferred to full-range motion, that exercise times could be greatly reduced, and that workouts could be performed far less often by focusing on intensity instead of duration.

The Golfer's Two-Minute Workout demonstrated how the strength gains from very brief static contraction workouts could translate into vastly improved drive distances and stamina, reduced handicaps, and other general improvements in a sport widely believed to be unaffected by muscular strength.

Now, *Power Factor Specialization: Chest & Arms* is going to prove something else that will startle bodybuilders, trainers, and exercise physiologists. Many of the exercises that are the bedrock of common strength training programs are grossly inefficient, nearly a total waste of time, including exercises on some of the most expensive equipment made.

By examining these exercises, we draw conclusions about which ones yield the most benefit. We then combine those exercises into specialized routines that target specific areas of the body. Those routines virtually guarantee unprecedented size and strength gains in the targeted muscle groups.

EXERCISING TO FAILURE

Here is something absolutely critical to remember while reading the next few chapters: *Any exercise can be done to failure*—even with a 1-pound weight! This means that when you want to exercise your chest, for example, you might choose dumbbell flies or you might choose decline bench presses. In either case you can perform the exercise for several repetitions until you are at the point where you cannot complete one more rep. You are at *failure*. At the end of either such exercise you might think that you have done a thorough job of overloading your chest muscles and of stimulating new size and strength growth. You haven't. One of those exercises is very inefficient, so inefficient that it's a waste of your time and effort—even though you performed it to failure! That's right, even though you went all out, felt the burn, got a pump, and endured the pain that is supposed to give the gain, you wasted your time and effort on an exercise that barely tapped the power of your chest! And we can prove it!

Since all exercises can induce muscular failure, we wanted to measure to determine whether or not different exercises caused failure at different rates. The measurement of intensity (Power Factor) for each exercise was taken over a 60-second period. The test subjects performed each exercise with sufficient weight to cause failure within 60 seconds of exercise. In the event that they hit failure before 60 seconds, they could pause, then grind out a few more reps until the 60 seconds had fully elapsed. In short, they engaged in the maximum amount of output that they could for each exercise.

For example, the Nautilus pullover machine might induce failure in a test subject using 100 pounds and completing 20 reps in 1 minute. This would yield an apparent (we'll discuss the term *apparent* in a moment) Power Factor of 2,000 pounds per minute of chest overload. The same test subject might induce failure on the incline bench press using 135 pounds for 19 repetitions. This would yield a Power Factor of 2,565 pounds per minute of chest overload (a 28 percent increase). In each case the subject was unable to complete another repetition, yet one of the exercises involved 28 percent more output from the same muscle group. So the question is, why perform an exercise that delivers less intensity of overload to the muscle group you are targeting?

RATING THE EXERCISES

You will see that all exercises are not created equal. Some are highly effective at involving all of a muscle group and generating maximal overload. Others generate only a fraction of a muscle's total capacity for output. It is a well-established fact that intensity of muscular overload is the single most important factor in triggering the growth of muscle. The oft-used analogy of the sprinter's thighs versus the marathoner's thighs is a clear example of how high intensity muscular output develops thick, powerful muscles compared to the results of lower intensities of output. The evidence for the primacy of high intensity is so overwhelming, as found in both our own previous books and every respectable journal of physiology, that it is hardly necessary to make the case again. But just wait until you run into that guy in the gym who insists that some exercise that we have identified as low intensity is really a great way to isolate part of a muscle. Such arguments would be amusing if they didn't cause so many bodybuilders to waste years of training. "Isolating part of a muscle" is a little like running with one nostril plugged in an attempt to isolate one lung. Why? Even if it worked to some degree, do you know anyone who wants 80 percent of his triceps to wither while the isolated 20 percent shows improvement? Show us an MRI of an exercise that activates one head out of the three heads of the triceps and we'll show you an exercise to avoid like the plague.

This book shows you how to use the most efficient exercises to ensure high intensity of muscular overload and how to engineer your chest and arm workouts to ensure progressive overload.

These two elements combine to make the most potent routines possible for chest and arm development.

CHEST EXERCISES

Please remember that the test subjects performing this exercise and all the others in the study were going all out and trying to lift the heaviest weight possible for as many repetitions as possible in one full minute. When they finished this exercise, they were at the point of not being able to complete another rep and would have had to take a substantial rest if they were going to attempt another (lower-intensity, no doubt) set of repetitions. Sound familiar? This is the way 99 percent of the people in a gym train. The enlightened 1 percent train smart instead.

Straight-Arm Pullover

The straight-arm pullover averaged a Power Factor of 563. By itself, that number doesn't mean very much. You can see how little that is compared to the full output capacity of the chest muscles by looking at the graph for this exercise. This pie graph illustrates that the relative overload to the chest muscles was 12.8 percent of what the chest muscles were capable of in the number-one high-intensity chest exercise.

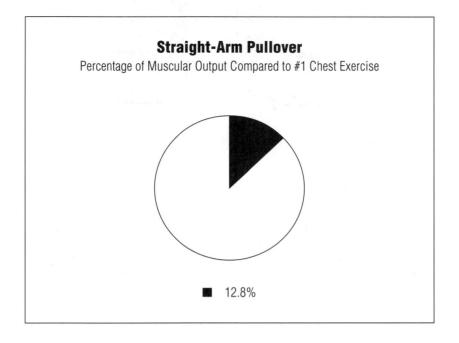

Straight-Arm Pullover

Percentage of Muscular Output Compared to #1 Chest Exercise

■ 12.8%

Nautilus Machine Pullover

Here's a little bombshell for you: when using Nautilus and other types of machines, "100 pounds" does not equal 100 pounds. We have had a suspicion about this for some time. Think about it—how is it that a weight stack can be connected to several pulleys that reduce the effort needed to raise it (thanks, Mr. Archimedes) yet still be called the same weight no matter how many pulleys are involved? It can't. Recognizing this, we did something that, it seems, nobody has ever thought to do before. We measured the actual amount of weight that a bodybuilder is lifting when the Nautilus machine or the cable pulley machine says "50 pounds" or "100 pounds."

Using a digital scale that is used in fishing tournaments, we compared the weight claimed on the weight stack to the actual weight necessary to move the apparatus. So what do 100 Nautilus pounds weigh? It varied between 37 and 50 pounds! That's right, the high intensity you think you are getting with this machine is 50 to 60 percent lower! Interestingly, of the four Nautilus machines we tested, the pullover machine was the only one that showed a significant variation of force throughout the range of

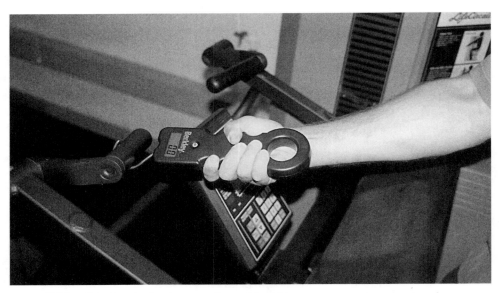

With a digital scale that is normally used in fishing tournaments, we compared the weight claimed on the weight stack to the actual weight necessary to move the apparatus.

motion. The shaped cam was supposed to be designed to significantly alter the force curve in order to correspond with human kinesiology. On three of the machines we measured, the difference was too small (1 to 2 pounds of 50) to make any difference at all.

Without knowing the real truth of how much overload this machine delivers, Power Factor trainees would make a calculation

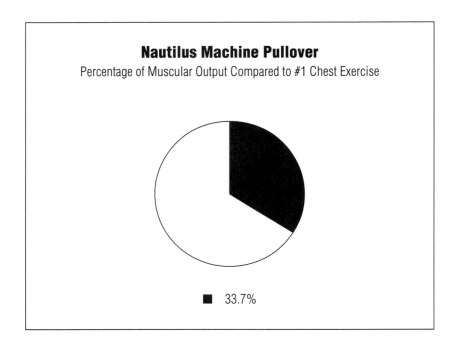

Nautilus Machine Pullover

Percentage of Muscular Output Compared to #1 Chest Exercise

■ 33.7%

that would put the pullover machine near the top of the chest exercise list, with a Power Factor of about 77 percent of full chest intensity. In reality it is only 33.7 percent, not very good for a multi-thousand-dollar machine.

Flat Bench Cable Crossover

The flat bench cable crossover is another exercise that uses a "machine" in the form of a pulley system. These pulley machines are in every gym in the world, and there must be thousands of different manufacturers. Fortunately, they all use approximately the same design, so our measurements should be a pretty good yardstick.

The true weight on this machine was only about 65 percent of what the weight stack indicated.

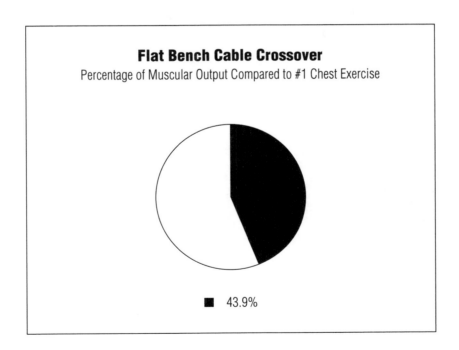

Flat Bench Cable Crossover

Percentage of Muscular Output Compared to #1 Chest Exercise

■ 43.9%

Dumbbell Fly

The dumbbell fly is a very common chest exercise that works the pecs at about 45 percent of the intensity of what they are capable. This means there is no such thing as "high-intensity" dumbbell flies relative to other chest exercises. Think about that, and think about how many millions of man-hours have been wasted in gyms this century performing low-intensity exercises like this.

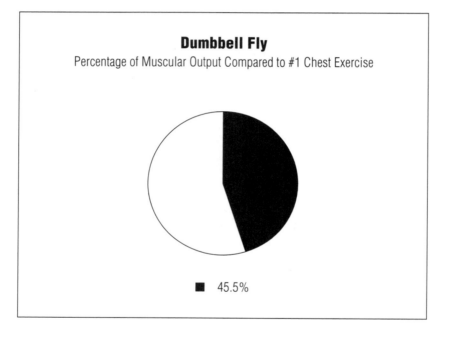

Dumbbell Fly

Percentage of Muscular Output Compared to #1 Chest Exercise

■ 45.5%

Incline Barbell Press

The incline barbell press is our first bench press exercise, and now we finally see the intensity go over the 50 percent mark. Because of the incline, this exercise partially involves the shoulder muscles and a little less of the chest muscles.

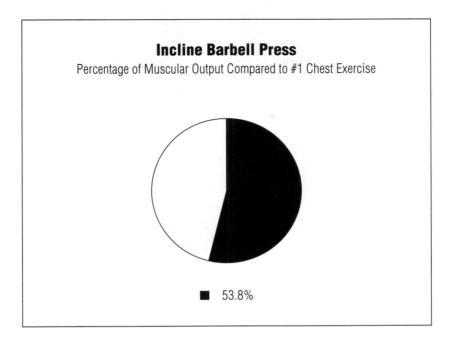

Incline Barbell Press

Percentage of Muscular Output Compared to #1 Chest Exercise

■ 53.8%

Nautilus 10-Degree Chest Machine

The Nautilus 10-degree chest machine yielded a true weight of 52 percent of the expected weight. We measured this machine by selecting "100 pounds" on the weight stack, which should deliver 50 pounds to each arm of the machine. Instead we measured 26 pounds each throughout the range of motion of the machine.

We cannot overstate how important this piece of knowledge is. Without knowing the truth that was revealed by the scale, this exercise would appear to be the most intense chest exercise that we tested! In reality it is only in the middle of the pack, at 57.5 percent of possible overload intensity. A bodybuilder could grind away with this machine for months and never know he was cheating himself out of progress every single workout.

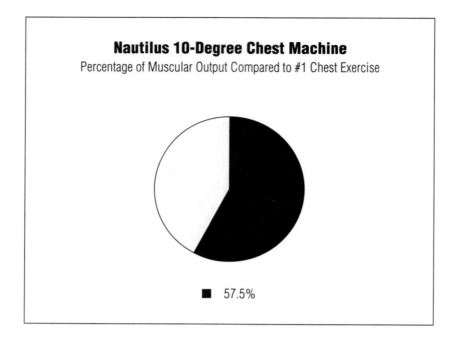

Nautilus 10-Degree Chest Machine

Percentage of Muscular Output Compared to #1 Chest Exercise

■   57.5%

Unilateral High Pulley Cable Crossover

Even with a high pulley system that delivered only about 63 percent of the indicated weight, this exercise generated a respectable intensity.

Note: With this and all other unilateral, or one-handed, exercises the Power Factor numbers were doubled to obtain an "apples to apples" comparison. For example, this exercise generated a Power Factor of 1,540 pounds per minute using one arm. That number was doubled to 3,080 in order to compare it with the other chest exercises that involved using both arms at the same time. So while this exercise generated a very high overload, it actually requires twice the exercise time in order to work both sides of the chest.

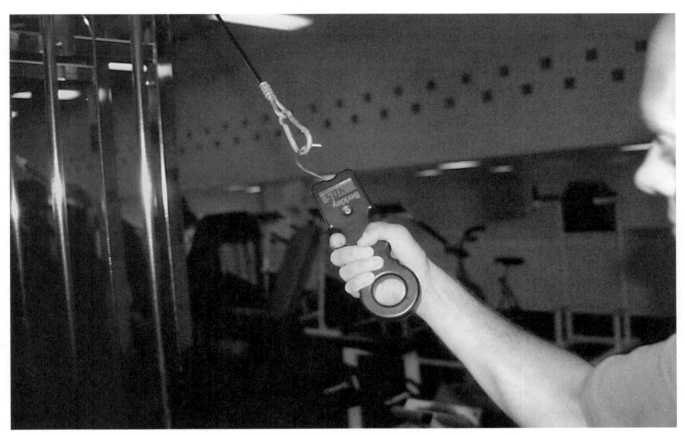

The high pulley delivered only 63 percent of the indicated weight.

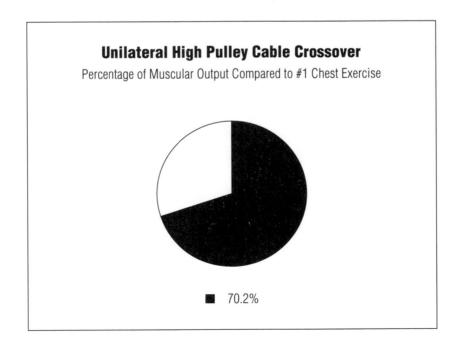

Unilateral High Pulley Cable Crossover

Percentage of Muscular Output Compared to #1 Chest Exercise

■ 70.2%

Bilateral High Pulley Cable Crossover

Here we see that there was actually a gain of efficiency and intensity by performing this exercise with both arms simultaneously. This movement jumped into third place with 91.5 percent of possible intensity, and that's after adjusting for the actual weight supplied by the pulleys.

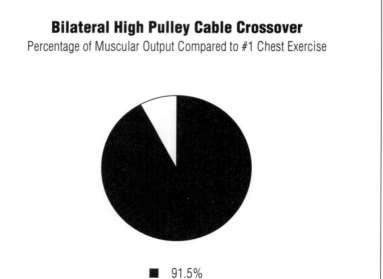

Bilateral High Pulley Cable Crossover

Percentage of Muscular Output Compared to #1 Chest Exercise

■ 91.5%

Decline Barbell Bench Press

The decline barbell bench press is a great chest exercise. We would not be surprised if this movement was the number-one exercise for some bodybuilders. The 97 percent figure is so close that it could easily go the other way. We recommend experimenting with this movement to see if you are one of the people who can grind out more intensity with this movement than any other.

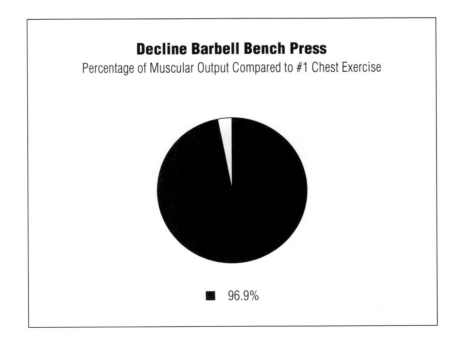

Decline Barbell Bench Press

Percentage of Muscular Output Compared to #1 Chest Exercise

■ 96.9%

Barbell Bench Press

The barbell bench press is the king of chest exercises. Isn't it interesting that this simple exercise, done with inexpensive equipment, does more to promote muscle growth than an exercise done with expensively engineered machinery?

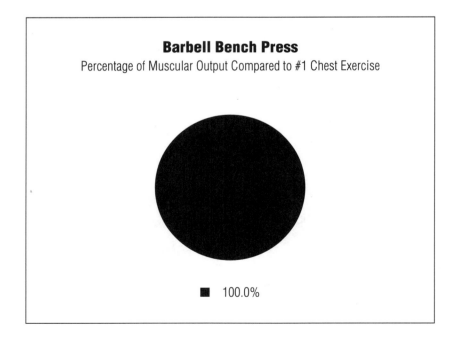

Barbell Bench Press

Percentage of Muscular Output Compared to #1 Chest Exercise

■ 100.0%

At a Glance

The Chest Exercises at a Glance graph shows you a comparison of the Power Factors of all of the most popular chest exercises. You can see immediately the futility of many of them. When you understand the critical role of intensity in generating muscle growth, it's clear that an exercise that delivers more intensity is better than one that delivers less. For example, if you were capable of doing a full set of bench press repetitions with 200 pounds, performing straight-arm barbell pullovers would be the equivalent overload of performing that same bench press set with only 26 pounds! How would that force growth of your chest muscles? Why would they need to grow when they are already capable of a higher intensity output? They won't grow—they'll wither!

When you really understand this you'll realize just how important these findings are to productive exercise.

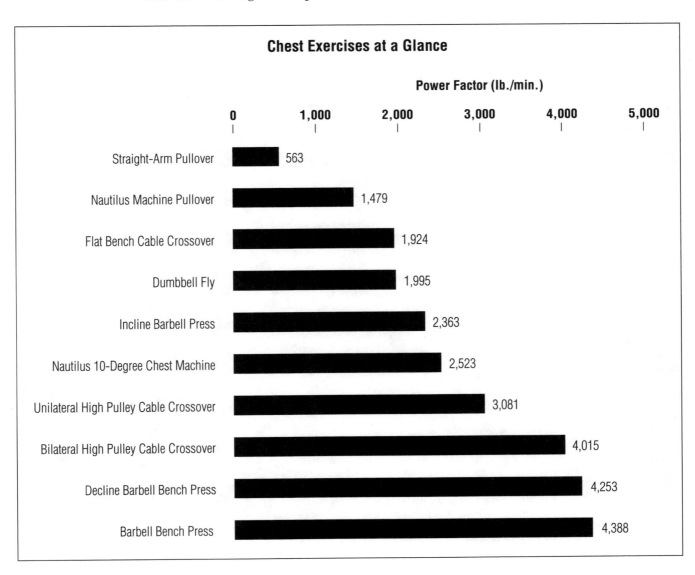

Chest Exercises at a Glance

Power Factor (lb./min.)

Exercise	Power Factor
Straight-Arm Pullover	563
Nautilus Machine Pullover	1,479
Flat Bench Cable Crossover	1,924
Dumbbell Fly	1,995
Incline Barbell Press	2,363
Nautilus 10-Degree Chest Machine	2,523
Unilateral High Pulley Cable Crossover	3,081
Bilateral High Pulley Cable Crossover	4,015
Decline Barbell Bench Press	4,253
Barbell Bench Press	4,388

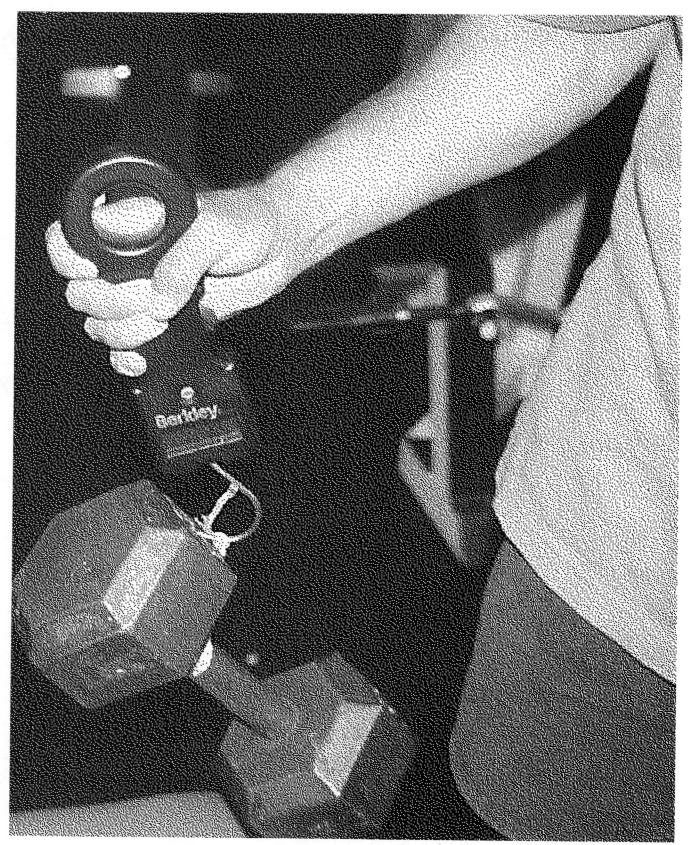

Free weights measured exactly as advertised

6

Rating the Arm Exercises

These exercises were measured with the same methods and procedures described in Chapter 5.

TRICEPS EXERCISES

High Pulley Pressdown

The high pulley pressdown could be the most common triceps exercise in any gym. Virtually every exercise book ever written on the subject of arm training recommends pressdowns as a premium triceps exercise. Even we were surprised at just how dismal this movement's performance was.

This exercise yielded less than 25 percent of what was possible with the triceps muscles. Once again, the trainee would be oblivious to this poor performance, which is largely due to the mechanical advantage of the pulleys' reducing the real weight to a fraction of the indicated weight. Even vigilant Power Factor trainees, who would record the weight used and the number of repetitions, would believe this exercise is more intense than it really is.

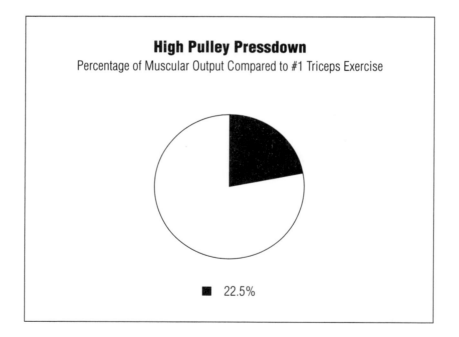

High Pulley Pressdown

Percentage of Muscular Output Compared to #1 Triceps Exercise

■ 22.5%

Lying Low Pulley Triceps Curl

The lying low pulley triceps curl is another example of a common exercise that scored very low.

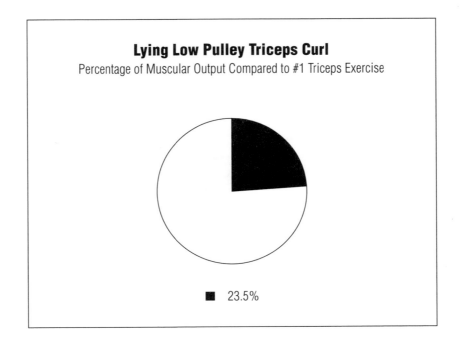

Lying Low Pulley Triceps Curl
Percentage of Muscular Output Compared to #1 Triceps Exercise

■ 23.5%

Nautilus Triceps Machine

Once again, rather than take information on faith, we took the time to measure the exact amount of force required to move this piece of equipment at various settings. Setting the machine at "100 pounds," we took a measurement from one side, which you would expect to be exactly 50 pounds. It was 24 pounds. Moreover, it was 24 pounds no matter where in the range we measured. With this Nautilus machine, a 100-pound triceps exercise is actually a 48-pound triceps exercise!

All that money and engineering for 27.6 percent of potential intensity.

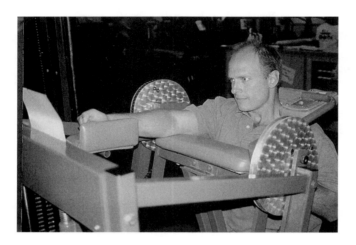

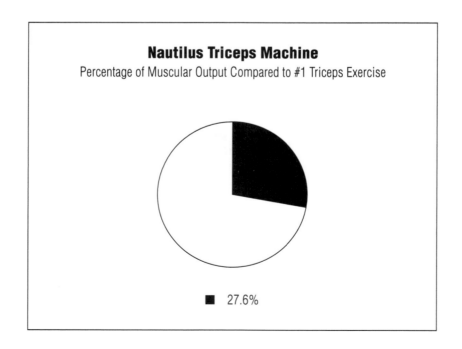

Nautilus Triceps Machine

Percentage of Muscular Output Compared to #1 Triceps Exercise

■ 27.6%

Bent-Over Dumbbell Triceps Extension

The bent-over dumbbell triceps extension is another common exercise that yields less than one-third of what the triceps can do.

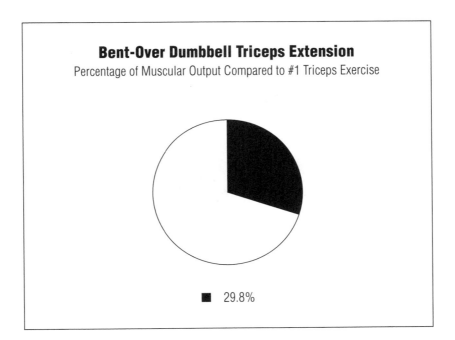

Bent-Over Dumbbell Triceps Extension

Percentage of Muscular Output Compared to #1 Triceps Exercise

■ 29.8%

Standing One-Arm Dumbbell Triceps Extension

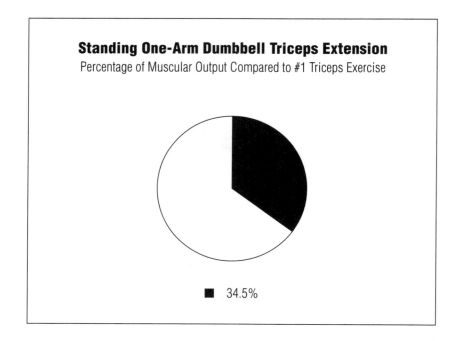

Standing One-Arm Dumbbell Triceps Extension

Percentage of Muscular Output Compared to #1 Triceps Exercise

■ 34.5%

Standing Barbell Triceps Extension

Once again we see that using a barbell garners better results than using a single dumbbell at a time.

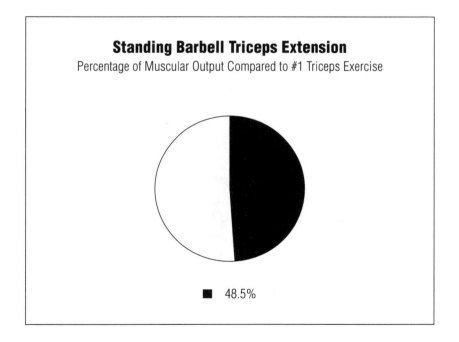

Standing Barbell Triceps Extension
Percentage of Muscular Output Compared to #1 Triceps Exercise

■ 48.5%

Seated Barbell Triceps Extension

The seated barbell triceps extension was the first exercise that made it to half of the intensity that the triceps are capable of generating.

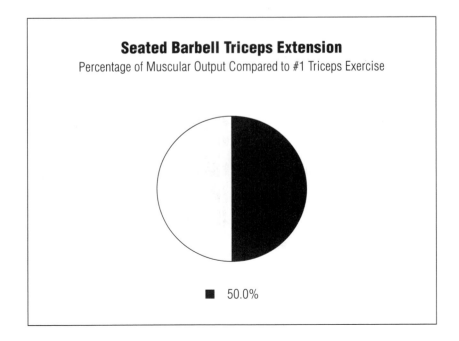

Seated Barbell Triceps Extension

Percentage of Muscular Output Compared to #1 Triceps Exercise

■ 50.0%

Close-Grip Bench Press

It came as no surprise to us that the close-grip bench press scored extremely high on the intensity measurement. We have been recommending this exercise for many years. In fact, we fully expected this to be the number-one exercise. It came very close. And what's more, it is possible to increase intensity even further using the next exercise.

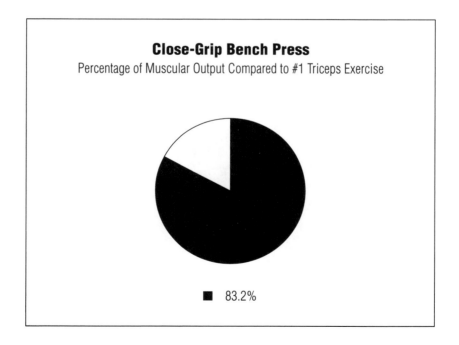

Close-Grip Bench Press

Percentage of Muscular Output Compared to #1 Triceps Exercise

■ 83.2%

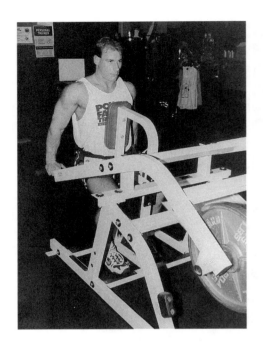

Hammer Strength Dip Machine

Hammer Strength makes great equipment. In case you're wondering, we used the scale to test this machine and other Hammer Strength machines. In all cases the amount of weight delivered to the user was the indicated weight or slightly more. We are of the opinion that if Hammer Strength equipment was designed with a range-limiting mechanism it would be the finest equipment you could own.

If your gym has one of these machines, we recommend that you use it for your triceps training. If it does not, the close-grip bench press will be more than sufficient. In fact, performed in the strongest range of motion only, the close-grip bench press will far surpass even the Hammer Strength dip machine, which cannot be reliably restricted in range.

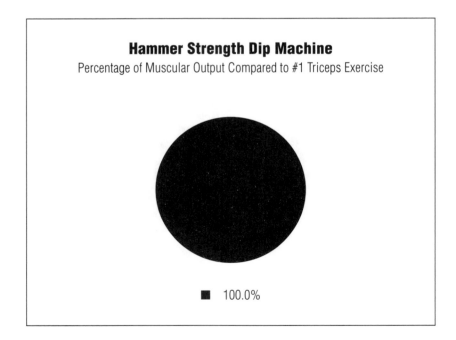

At a Glance

Looking at the Triceps Exercises at a Glance graph, once again we see an enormous disparity between the worst exercises and the best exercises.

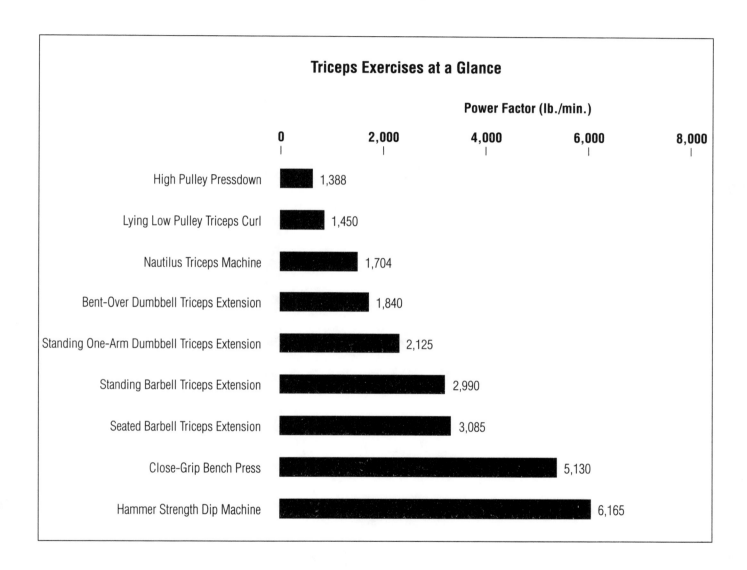

Triceps Exercises at a Glance

Power Factor (lb./min.)

Exercise	Power Factor
High Pulley Pressdown	1,388
Lying Low Pulley Triceps Curl	1,450
Nautilus Triceps Machine	1,704
Bent-Over Dumbbell Triceps Extension	1,840
Standing One-Arm Dumbbell Triceps Extension	2,125
Standing Barbell Triceps Extension	2,990
Seated Barbell Triceps Extension	3,085
Close-Grip Bench Press	5,130
Hammer Strength Dip Machine	6,165

BICEPS EXERCISES

The biceps exercises generally involved less variation. However, our measurements still made it easy to determine which exercises were the very best.

Standing Low Pulley Curl

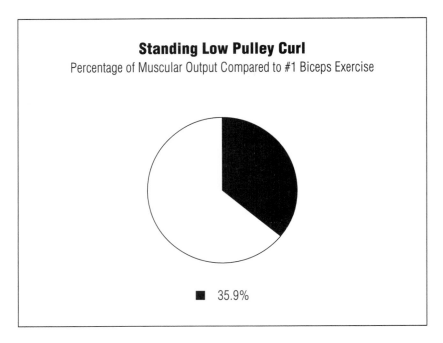

Standing Low Pulley Curl
Percentage of Muscular Output Compared to #1 Biceps Exercise

■ 35.9%

Seated Scott Dumbbell Curl

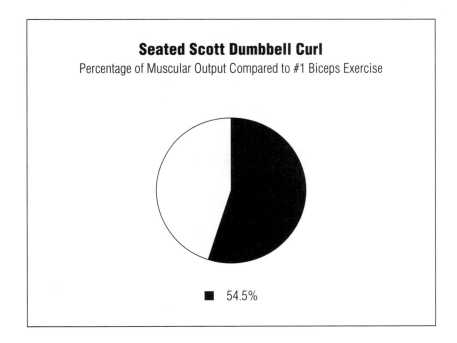

Seated Scott Dumbbell Curl

Percentage of Muscular Output Compared to #1 Biceps Exercise

■ 54.5%

Lying Dumbbell Curl

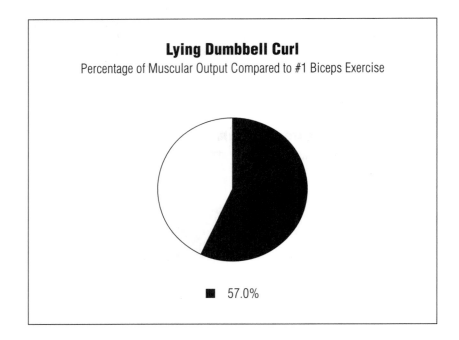

Lying Dumbbell Curl

Percentage of Muscular Output Compared to #1 Biceps Exercise

■ 57.0%

Nautilus Machine Curl

Once again we took exact measurements to determine how much force was required to move this apparatus. Selecting "100 pounds" on the weight stack, we expected to measure 50 pounds on each side of the apparatus. In fact, we measured 25 pounds. Again, we stress that without having this knowledge, the Nautilus machine curl would appear to be the number-one biceps exercise. In fact, it fails to deliver even 60 percent of the overload intensity of the best biceps exercise.

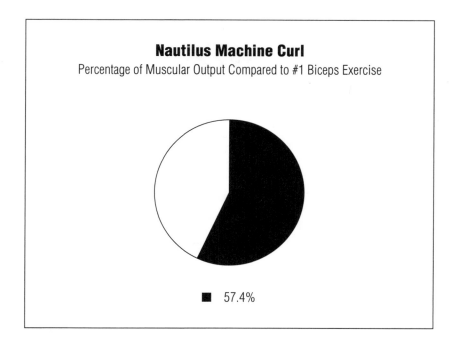

Nautilus Machine Curl

Percentage of Muscular Output Compared to #1 Biceps Exercise

■ 57.4%

Standing Scott Dumbbell Curl

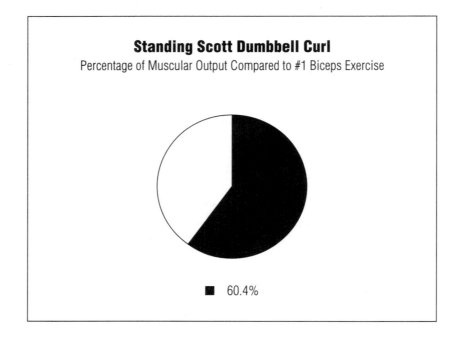

Standing Scott Dumbbell Curl

Percentage of Muscular Output Compared to #1 Biceps Exercise

■ 60.4%

Seated Scott Barbell Curl

This exercise, seated Scott barbell curl, and the next three, standing Scott barbell curl, standing dumbbell curl, and seated dumbbell curl, are so close together that they must be nearly identical in effect.

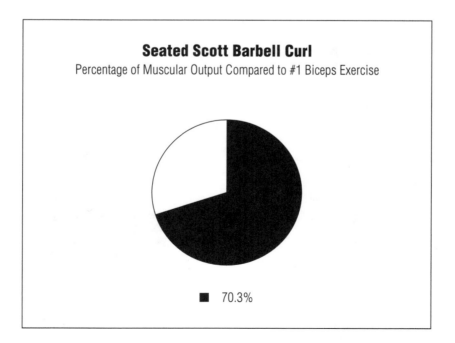

Seated Scott Barbell Curl

Percentage of Muscular Output Compared to #1 Biceps Exercise

■ 70.3%

Standing Scott Barbell Curl

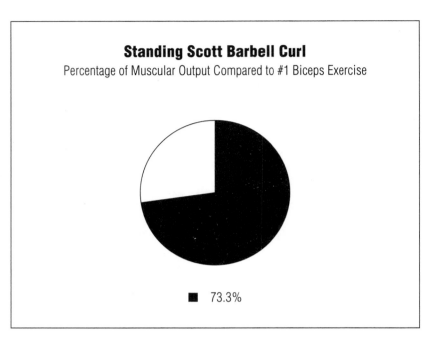

Standing Dumbbell Curl

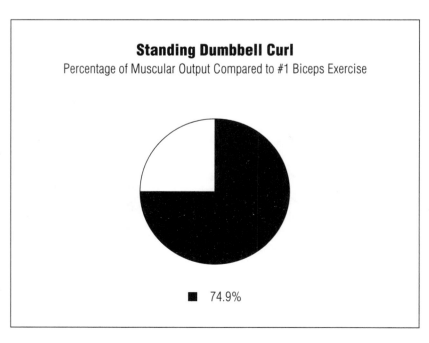

Seated Dumbbell Curl

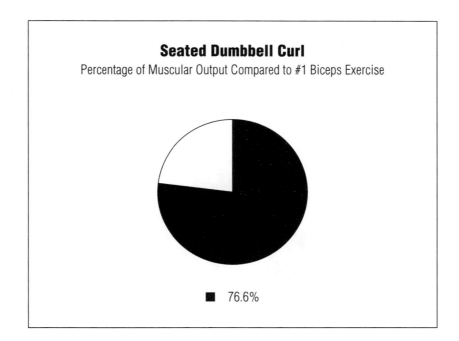

Seated Dumbbell Curl

Percentage of Muscular Output Compared to #1 Biceps Exercise

■ 76.6%

Hammer Strength Machine Biceps Curl

Once again, intensity took a big jump when we used a Hammer Strength machine.

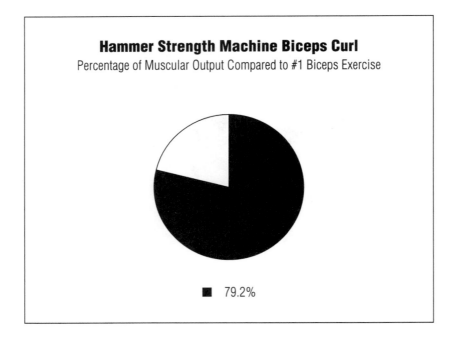

Hammer Strength Machine Biceps Curl

Percentage of Muscular Output Compared to #1 Biceps Exercise

■ 79.2%

Standing Barbell Curl

The standing barbell curl is a great exercise and could have been the number-one exercise except for one element: it uses a full range of motion. The *seated* barbell curl is, in effect, a strong-range exercise because the bar cannot descend below the level of the lap. The more the range is restricted, the heavier the weight is that can be used and, therefore, the higher the intensity.

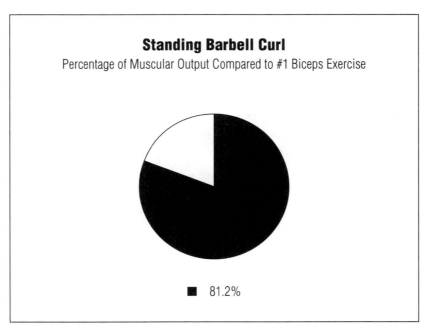

Standing Barbell Curl

Percentage of Muscular Output Compared to #1 Biceps Exercise

■ 81.2%

Seated Barbell Curl

As stated above, the seated barbell curl probably scores as high as it does because of the restricted range of motion implicit in its operation. In fact, in the absence of a training partner or a power rack, this exercise is an excellent way to perform a strong-range biceps exercise.

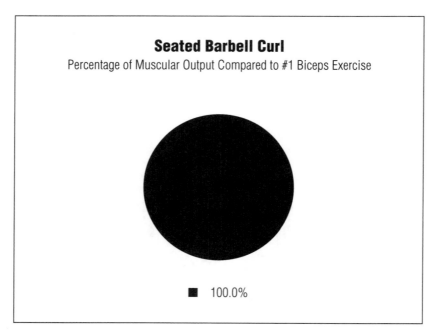

Seated Barbell Curl

Percentage of Muscular Output Compared to #1 Biceps Exercise

■ 100.0%

At a Glance

Looking at the Biceps Exercises at a Glance graph, it is interesting to note the one exercise that partially limits the range of motion, seated barbell curl, is the exercise that stands alone in the measure of intensity. Also note that when so many exercises score close together, it behooves each individual bodybuilder to perform experimentation to determine which of these exercises generates the highest overload for him.

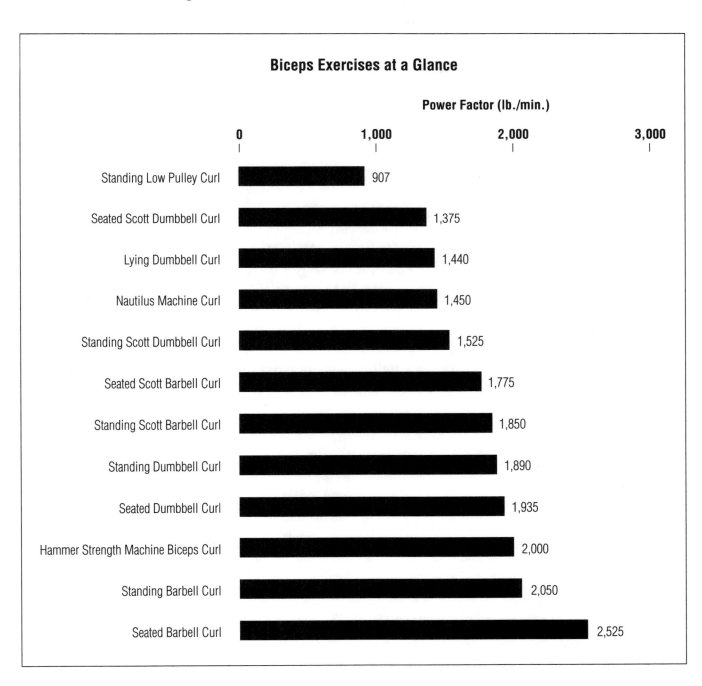

Biceps Exercises at a Glance

Power Factor (lb./min.)

Exercise	Power Factor
Standing Low Pulley Curl	907
Seated Scott Dumbbell Curl	1,375
Lying Dumbbell Curl	1,440
Nautilus Machine Curl	1,450
Standing Scott Dumbbell Curl	1,525
Seated Scott Barbell Curl	1,775
Standing Scott Barbell Curl	1,850
Standing Dumbbell Curl	1,890
Seated Dumbbell Curl	1,935
Hammer Strength Machine Biceps Curl	2,000
Standing Barbell Curl	2,050
Seated Barbell Curl	2,525

FOREARM EXERCISES

Because there are so many muscles in the forearms, the results of our test of each forearm exercise need to be carefully analyzed in order to find the best combination of forearm exercises.

Seated Low Pulley Reverse Wrist Curl

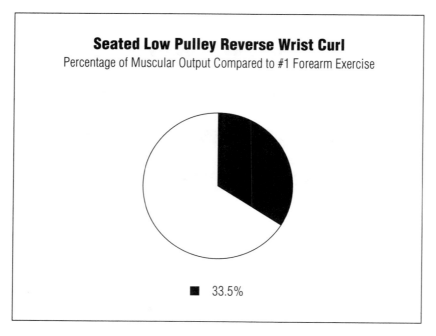

Seated Low Pulley Reverse Wrist Curl
Percentage of Muscular Output Compared to #1 Forearm Exercise

■ 33.5%

Seated Low Pulley Wrist Curl

Once again, we see that exercises involving the pulley are far less efficient than they appear to be.

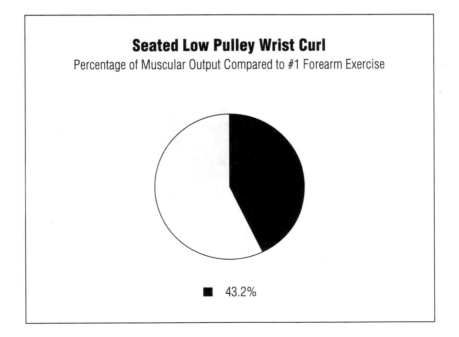

Seated Low Pulley Wrist Curl

Percentage of Muscular Output Compared to #1 Forearm Exercise

■ 43.2%

Standing Dumbbell Reverse Curl

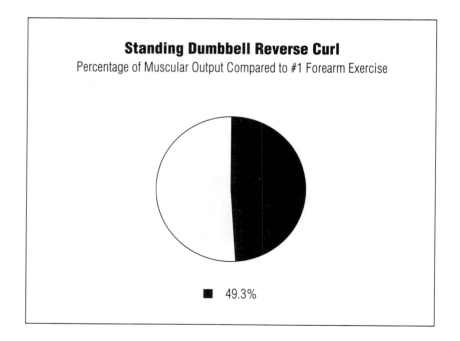

Standing Dumbbell Reverse Curl

Percentage of Muscular Output Compared to #1 Forearm Exercise

■   49.3%

Standing Barbell Reverse Curl

Despite the standing barbell reverse curl's being only half the intensity of the wrist curl, it is actually quite a productive exercise for the associated muscles of the forearm.

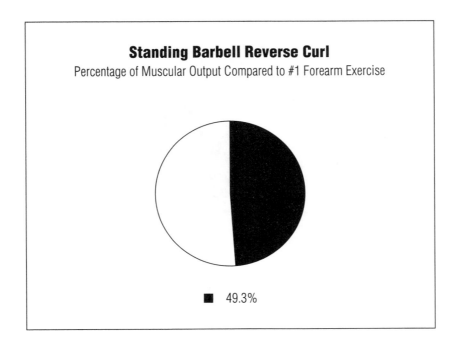

Standing Barbell Reverse Curl
Percentage of Muscular Output Compared to #1 Forearm Exercise

■ 49.3%

Seated Barbell Reverse Wrist Curl

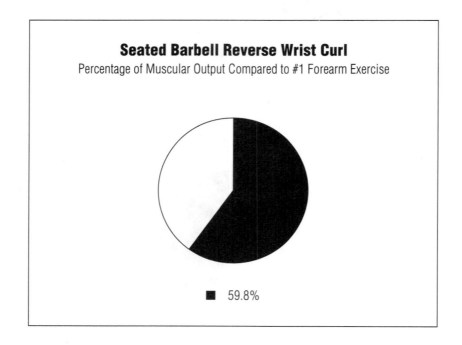

Seated Barbell Reverse Wrist Curl
Percentage of Muscular Output Compared to #1 Forearm Exercise

■ 59.8%

Seated Dumbbell Reverse Wrist Curl

This is another good exercise; in fact, it is the number-one reverse wrist curl.

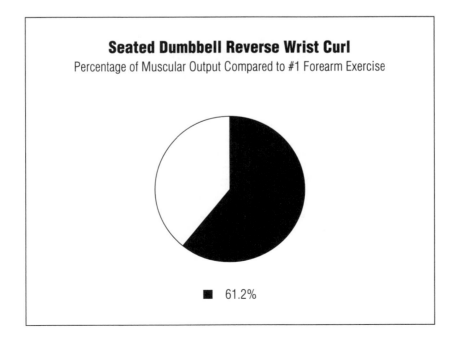

Seated Dumbbell Reverse Wrist Curl

Percentage of Muscular Output Compared to #1 Forearm Exercise

■ 61.2%

Seated Barbell Wrist Curl

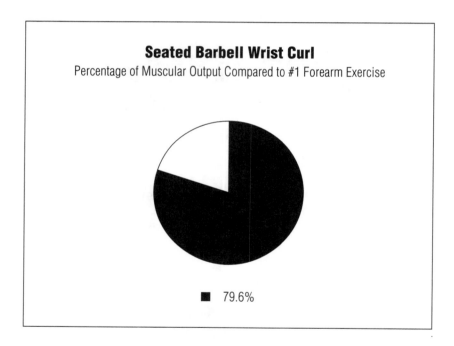

Seated Barbell Wrist Curl

Percentage of Muscular Output Compared to #1 Forearm Exercise

■   79.6%

Seated Dumbbell Wrist Curl

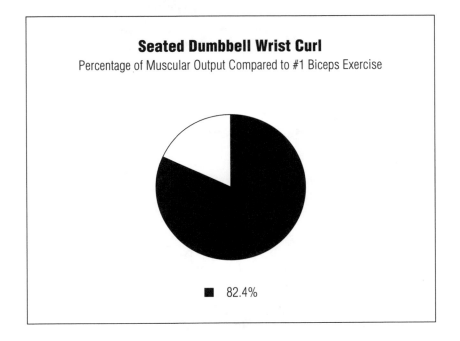

Seated Dumbbell Wrist Curl

Percentage of Muscular Output Compared to #1 Biceps Exercise

■ 82.4%

Standing Barbell Wrist Curl Behind Back

The rating for this exercise was a pleasant surprise. The standing barbell wrist curl behind back is a little obscure, and it was very nice to discover such a boon. It's quite rare to see a bodybuilder performing wrist curls in this fashion, but let's hope that changes.

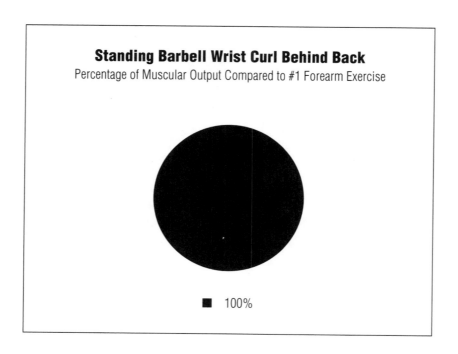

Standing Barbell Wrist Curl Behind Back

Percentage of Muscular Output Compared to #1 Forearm Exercise

■   100%

At a Glance

The evidence, as seen on the Forearm Exercises at a Glance graph, speaks for itself.

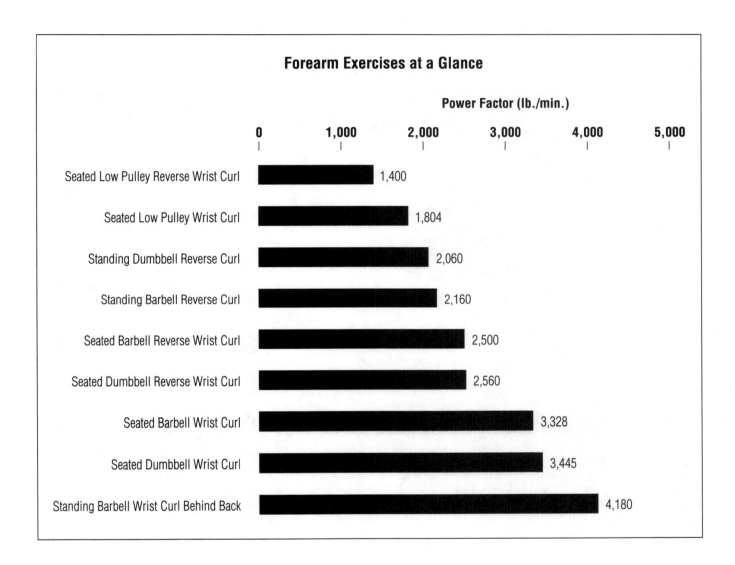

Forearm Exercises at a Glance

Power Factor (lb./min.)

Exercise	Power Factor
Seated Low Pulley Reverse Wrist Curl	1,400
Seated Low Pulley Wrist Curl	1,804
Standing Dumbbell Reverse Curl	2,060
Standing Barbell Reverse Curl	2,160
Seated Barbell Reverse Wrist Curl	2,500
Seated Dumbbell Reverse Wrist Curl	2,560
Seated Barbell Wrist Curl	3,328
Seated Dumbbell Wrist Curl	3,445
Standing Barbell Wrist Curl Behind Back	4,180

Specialized Chest Routines

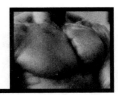

To say that the information in Chapters 5 and 6 is interesting is to understate the case considerably. It is now plain to see that using training machines costing, collectively, hundreds of thousands of dollars is no guarantee whatsoever of a productive workout. Further, some of the most popular free-weight exercises are similarly inefficient, to the point of being useless.

But now that we enlightened bodybuilders have this information at our fingertips, we are able to create the most productive chest and arm training routines possible. Thanks to the Power Factor method of quantifying and tracking exercise, we can engineer both intensity and progressive overload into every workout.

Over the years we have seen a broad variation in exercise response and tolerance in individuals. For this reason, we are providing workouts that stimulate muscle growth by taxing both short-duration alpha strength and longer-duration beta strength. Record your results on the Workout Record form (see Chapter 9, "Tracking Your Progress").

HIGH ALPHA STRENGTH CHEST WORKOUTS

Chest Alpha Strength Workout 1

Select a weight that represents 75 to 90 percent of your one-rep maximum in the bench press. We cannot stress enough that performing this exercise in the strongest range of motion will yield enormously greater benefits than would performing this exercise in the conventional full range. This has been proven by tens of thousands of Power Factor trainees and thousands more Static Contraction trainees.

    1 set of strong-range bench presses to failure

Your muscles are capable of handling so much more weight in the strong-range bench press that you will require a power rack for extra safety.

Using strong-range reps, which are short and quick, you will probably reach failure within 30 repetitions or so.

Chest Alpha Strength Workout 2

For each of the exercises of Workouts 2 and 3, select a weight that represents 75 to 90 percent of your one-rep maximum.

1 set of strong-range high pulley cable crossovers to failure
1 set of strong-range decline barbell bench presses to failure
1 set of strong-range barbell bench presses to failure

You will require a brief rest between these exercises. Most people find 30 seconds to 2 minutes adequate. However, you should always be mindful that while the clock is ticking your Power Factor is 0 pounds per minute, and that will bring down the intensity of your workout. Rest just long enough to recover but no more. Note that when we say *to failure* we mean to continue grinding out repetitions until you cannot do another—even if it means 40, 50, or 60 repetitions. Use this as a guide for your next workout. For example, if you perform 60 repetitions with 200 pounds, use 275 pounds next time so that the repetitions are reduced.

Chest Alpha Strength Workout 3

    2 sets of strong-range high pulley cable crossovers to failure
    2 sets of strong-range decline barbell bench presses to
       failure
    2 sets of strong-range barbell bench presses to failure

You will require a brief rest between sets as well as between these exercises. This workout begins to tap beta strength. Some trainees will respond best to this workout, while others will never make better progress than when using a single set as in Workout 1. Be sure to do some experimentation with these workouts to determine which one best suits the adaptation and recovery ability of your body.

HIGH BETA STRENGTH CHEST WORKOUTS

Once again, you'll achieve the best results with these workouts while using weights that are 75 to 90 percent of your one-rep maximum in the strongest range of motion. These beta strength workouts take longer and are designed to tap the endurance reserves that are contained within your muscles. These workouts are best suited to those individuals who, after only a brief rest, can duplicate their last set, weight for weight and rep for rep. Such individuals have higher than normal beta strength.

Chest Beta Strength Workout 1

4 sets of barbell bench presses to failure

Strictly speaking, not all of these sets need to be done to failure. Once you have a good feel for where your "sweet spot" is located, you may find your best results by increasing the weight on each set and going to failure only on the final set.

Chest Beta Strength Workout 2

> 3 or 4 sets of strong-range high pulley cable crossovers to failure
>
> 3 or 4 sets of strong-range barbell decline bench presses to failure
>
> 3 or 4 sets of strong-range barbell bench presses to failure

Once again, not all of the sets need to be done to failure. It's just that when you go to failure you know that you gave it "everything in the tank" before giving up. That keeps you honest. This workout takes much longer to perform and seriously taps the reserves of strength contained in your muscles. We recommend this routine only as a last resort for that minority of individuals whose bodies are not responding to the other workouts we have provided.

RECORD KEEPING

You need to keep track of when you begin and end each workout. You also need to record the weight, sets, and reps for each exercise and the amount of time it took to complete each exercise. All of this is explained in detail in Chapter 9, "Tracking Your Progress."

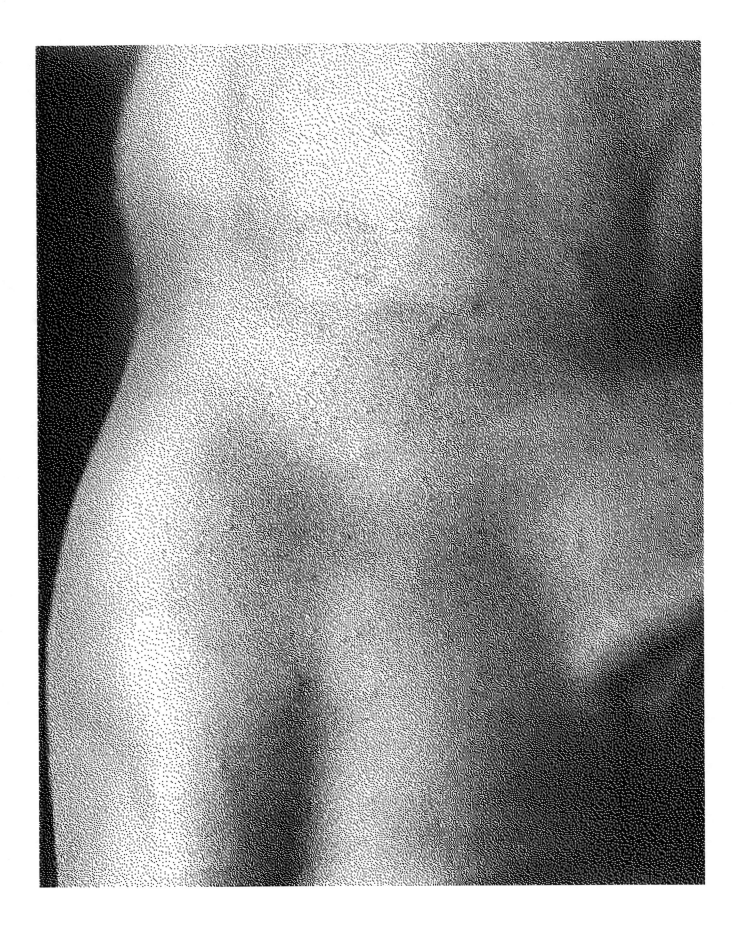

8

Specialized Arm Routines

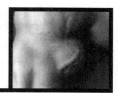

The major points we made at the beginning of Chapter 7 bear repeating. Specifically, since we now know that some exercises are far more productive than others, it only makes sense to design workouts that capitalize on the use of them. Further, if we keep strict track of the intensity of overload in each workout, we are able to design future workouts that are certain to be productive.

In arm training, as with that of any other muscle of the body, we can benefit by using workouts predesigned to stimulate overload in both alpha strength and beta strength. Record your results on the Workout Record form (see Chapter 9, "Tracking Your Progress").

HIGH ALPHA STRENGTH TRICEPS WORKOUTS

Triceps Alpha Strength Workout 1

Select a weight that represents 75 to 90 percent of your one-rep maximum in the bench press. Again we stress that performing these exercises in the strongest range of motion will yield enormously greater benefits than would performing them in the conventional full range.

1 set of Hammer Strength machine dips or close-grip bench presses to failure

Using strong-range reps, which are short and quick, you will probably reach failure within 30 repetitions or so.

Triceps Alpha Strength Workout 2

For the exercises in Triceps Alpha Strength Workouts 2 and 3, select a weight that represents 75 to 90 percent of your one-rep maximum.

1 set of strong-range standing barbell triceps extensions

1 set of Hammer Strength machine dips or close-grip bench presses to failure

Note: If you have access to both a Hammer Strength machine and a bench press, perform a total of 3 sets using triceps extensions and close-grip bench presses followed by Hammer Strength machine dips.

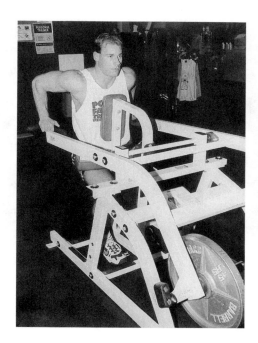

You will require a brief rest between these exercises. Most people find 30 seconds to 2 minutes adequate. However, you should always be mindful that while the clock is ticking your Power Factor is 0 pounds per minute, and that will bring down the intensity of your workout. Rest just long enough to recover but no more. Note that when we say *to failure* we mean to continue grinding out repetitions until you cannot do another—even if it means 40, 50, or 60 repetitions. Use this as a guide for your next workout. For example, if you perform 60 repetitions with 200 pounds, use 275 pounds next time so that the repetitions are reduced.

Triceps Alpha Strength Workout 3

2 sets of strong-range standing barbell triceps extensions

2 sets of Hammer Strength machine dips or close-grip bench presses to failure

Note: If you have access to both a Hammer Strength machine and a bench press, perform a total of 6 sets using triceps extensions and close-grip bench presses followed by Hammer Strength machine dips for 2 sets each.

You will require a brief rest between sets as well as between these exercises. This workout begins to tap into beta strength. Some trainees will respond best to this workout, while others will never make better progress than when using a single set as in Workout 1. Experiment with these workouts to determine which suits the adaptation and recovery ability of your body.

HIGH BETA STRENGTH TRICEPS WORKOUTS

Once again, the best results with all of these beta strength workouts will be achieved while using weights that are 75 to 90 percent of your one-rep maximum in the strongest range of motion. These workouts take longer and are designed to tap the endurance reserves that are contained within your muscles. Remember that these workouts are best suited to those individuals who after only a brief rest can duplicate their last set, weight for weight and rep for rep. Such individuals have higher than normal beta strength.

Triceps Beta Strength Workout 1

> 4 sets of close-grip bench presses or Hammer Strength
> machine dips to failure

Remember that not all of these sets need to be done to failure. Once you have a good feel for where your "sweet spot" is located, you may find your best results by increasing the weight on each set and going to failure only on the final set.

Triceps Beta Strength Workout 2

3 or 4 sets of strong-range seated barbell triceps extensions
3 or 4 sets of strong-range close-grip bench presses or
Hammer Strength machine dips to failure

Note: If you have both the bench press and the Hammer Strength dip machine, perform 3 or 4 sets on each for a total of 9 or 12 sets.

As we've said, going to failure ensures that you give it all you've got before giving up. This workout takes much longer to perform and seriously taps into the reserves of strength contained in your muscles. We would recommend this routine only as a last resort for that minority of individuals whose bodies are not responding to the other workouts we have provided.

RECORD KEEPING

As with your chest workouts, you need to keep track of when you begin and end each workout. You also need to record the weight, sets, and reps for each exercise and the amount of time it took to complete each exercise. This is explained in detail in Chapter 9, "Tracking Your Progress."

HIGH ALPHA STRENGTH BICEPS WORKOUTS

Select a weight that represents 75 to 90 percent of your one-rep maximum on the standing barbell curl. Record your results on the Workout Record form (see Chapter 9).

Biceps Alpha Strength Workout 1

1 set of seated barbell curls to failure

Note: If possible, have a training partner restrict your movement on this exercise to the top 20 percent of the range of motion. This will permit the use of heavier weights and increase the overload and the rate of muscle growth.

Using strong-range reps, which are short and quick, you will probably reach failure within 30 repetitions or so.

Biceps Alpha Strength Workout 2

For the exercises in Workout 2, select a weight that represents 75 to 90 percent of your one-rep maximum.

  2 sets of standing barbell curls to failure
  2 sets of seated barbell curls to failure

You will require a brief rest between sets as well as between these exercises. This workout begins to tap beta strength. Some trainees will respond best to this workout, while others will never make better progress than when using a single set as in Workout 1. Be sure to do some experimentation with these workouts to determine which one best suits the adaptation and recovery ability of your body.

HIGH BETA STRENGTH BICEPS WORKOUTS

Biceps Beta Strength Workout 1

  4 or 5 sets of standing barbell curls to failure
  4 or 5 sets of seated barbell curls to failure

Note: You can substitute curls on the Hammer Strength biceps curl machine for standing barbell curls or use them as an extra exercise in the beta workout.

Once you have a good feel for where your "sweet spot" is located, you may find your best results by increasing the weight on each set and going to failure only on the final set.

HIGH ALPHA STRENGTH FOREARM WORKOUTS

Forearm Alpha Strength Workout 1

Select a weight that represents 75 to 90 percent of your one-rep maximum on the wrist curl. These exercises (except reverse curls) involve so little range of motion that trying to "restrict" movement to the strongest range is meaningless. However, have a training partner limit your reverse curls to the top of the range.

1 set of standing barbell reverse curls to failure
1 set of seated dumbbell reverse wrist curls to failure
1 set of standing barbell wrist curls behind back to failure

Note: Best results are obtained using barbells and dumbbells that are cast in one piece and therefore do not spin as you curl them.

Forearm Alpha Strength Workout 2

For each exercise select a weight that represents 75 to 90 percent of your one-rep maximum.

2 sets of standing barbell reverse curls to failure
2 sets of seated dumbbell reverse wrist curls to failure
2 sets of standing barbell wrist curls behind back to failure

HIGH BETA STRENGTH FOREARM WORKOUTS

Forearm Beta Strength Workout 1

    4 sets of standing barbell reverse curls to failure
    4 sets of seated dumbbell reverse wrist curls to failure
    4 sets of standing barbell wrist curls behind back

Don't forget to keep track of when you begin and end each workout. You also need to record the weight, sets, and reps for each exercise and the amount of time it took to complete each exercise.

THE WINNING COMBINATION

The exercises in the workouts in Chapters 7 and 8 truly represent the cutting edge in exercise technology. These are the exercises that have been empirically proven to deliver the most focused overload to the muscles of the chest and arms. They are combined in a way that exhausts both the short-term and the long-term reserves in the muscles themselves. Further, because you measure each workout exactly, you are guaranteed the indispensable element of progressive overload every workout. All of these factors combine to make the most potent specialized routines possible.

FREQUENCY OF WORKOUTS

In a productive exercise regimen the frequency of training is always changing. It is impossible to have progressive overload on a workout-to-workout basis and maintain a fixed (for example, three days per week) schedule. That virtually every training program suggests a fixed schedule shows how irrational exercise science is.

You have to start somewhere, though, and we recommend you do your specialized chest workout on Mondays and your specialized arm workout on Thursdays.

That's only two workouts per week, and you can only maintain this pace for a short time. Within two to five weeks you will see your progress slow down or even stop. When it does, it is time to train only once per week: chest one week and arms the next week. If you still want to continue with only specialization routines, you will soon have to train once every nine, ten, or eleven days. By this time the muscular power in your chest and arms will be so great that it will seriously tax your systemic recovery ability and require long periods of rest from training. Please don't worry about losing what you have gained over a one- or two-week layoff. We have many testimonials of trainees taking two months or more off from training only to come back into the gym as strong or stronger than when they left.

Learn to use the charts and graphs in Chapter 9 and everything else will take care of itself.

9

Tracking Your Progress

The most significant ramification of the innovation of the Power Factor and Power Index is that for the first time in the history of strength training, we have the ability to provide a simple and mathematically precise indication of muscular output. Now you can objectively measure your progress. Theories, myths, folklore, and science can all be put to the ultimate laboratory tests: How much overload does it deliver to the muscles? Does it develop greater strength? How much? How fast?

And this is just the tip of the proverbial iceberg. Henceforth, every factor that contributes to or detracts from your progress can now also be measured. You will be able to accurately measure the effect of doing more or fewer reps, doing more or fewer sets, using heavier or lighter weight, doing longer or shorter workouts, taking extra days off in between workouts, using different supplements, varying other aspects of your diet, and more.

In the domain of bodybuilding, powerlifting, or any other form of strength training, such instant and precise assessment is nothing short of revolutionary! No longer is it necessary for the strength athlete to measure his progress by feel or instinct. And all the equipment you need to unleash this powerful new technology is a logbook and a stopwatch, common items in virtually every other sport and yet so crucial in determining and plotting progress.

KEEPING TRACK OF YOUR NUMBERS

During your Power Factor Specialization workouts you will record the time, sets, reps, and weight that you lifted on the Workout Record form. After you perform a workout you should record your results for each exercise on the Exercise Performance Record form. The only calculation you need to make on the Workout Record and Exercise Performance Record forms is the percentage of change from workout to workout. This is accomplished by this simple method:

1. New Number – Old Number = Difference
2. Difference ÷ Old Number × 100% = % Change

For example, suppose your Power Factor goes from 1,675 to 1,890. Find the percent of change:

1. 1,890 – 1,675 = 215
2. 215 ÷ 1,675 = .128 × 100% = 12.8%

Workout Record Form

As you perform your workout, all you need to do is keep track of how many minutes it takes to do each exercise, how much weight you're using, and how many reps and sets you do with each weight. Record this information on the Workout Record form.

1. Enter the time of day you begin your workout. This will be used to calculate your overall performance. In all cases you should be sure to fully warm up before starting the clock on your workout. You should first perform your warm-up, taking as long as you like, then start timing your Power Factor Training. Your warm-up should never be counted as part of your Power Factor. Doing so will lead to an incentive to use heavy weights too quickly, ultimately causing injury. Warm-up completely first, then start the clock.

2. Enter the time of day that you finish your workout.

WORKOUT RECORD

Date: **3** / **8** / **99**

Start Time: ❶ **10:10 A.M.**   Finish Time: ❷ **10:31 A.M.**   Total Time: ❸ **21 min.**

■ Exercise: **Standing Barbell Curl**

Weight Reps Sets	Weight Reps Sets	Weight Reps Sets	Weight Reps Sets	Weight Reps Sets	Weight Reps Sets
90 × **20** × **2**	× ×	× ×	× ×	× ×	× ×
❹ Subtotal = **3,600** lb.	Subtotal = lb.	Subtotal = lb.	Subtotal = lb.	Subtotal = lb.	Subtotal = lb.

Exercise 1:   Total Weight **3,600** lb.   Time: **9** min.   Power Factor **400** lb./min.   Power Index **1.4**
❺ ❻ ❼ ❽

■ Exercise:

Weight Reps Sets	Weight Reps Sets	Weight Reps Sets	Weight Reps Sets	Weight Reps Sets	Weight Reps Sets
× ×	× ×	× ×	× ×	× ×	× ×
Subtotal = lb.	Subtotal = lb.	Subtotal = lb.	Subtotal = lb.	Subtotal = lb.	Subtotal = lb.

Exercise 2:   Total Weight _____ lb.   Time: _____ min.   Power Factor _____ lb./min.   Power Index _____

■ Exercise: **Seated Barbell Curl**

Weight Reps Sets	Weight Reps Sets	Weight Reps Sets	Weight Reps Sets	Weight Reps Sets	Weight Reps Sets
100 × **20** × **1**	**110** × **17** × **1**	× ×	× ×	× ×	× ×
Subtotal = **2,000** lb.	Subtotal = **1,700** lb.	Subtotal = lb.	Subtotal = lb.	Subtotal = lb.	Subtotal = lb.

Exercise 3:   Total Weight **3,700** lb.   Time: **8¼** min.   Power Factor **448** lb./min.   Power Index **1.66**

■ Exercise:

Weight Reps Sets	Weight Reps Sets	Weight Reps Sets	Weight Reps Sets	Weight Reps Sets	Weight Reps Sets
× ×	× ×	× ×	× ×	× ×	× ×
Subtotal = lb.	Subtotal = lb.	Subtotal = lb.	Subtotal = lb.	Subtotal = lb.	Subtotal = lb.

Exercise 4:   Total Weight _____ lb.   Time: _____ min.   Power Factor _____ lb./min.   Power Index _____

■ Exercise:

Weight Reps Sets	Weight Reps Sets	Weight Reps Sets	Weight Reps Sets	Weight Reps Sets	Weight Reps Sets
× ×	× ×	× ×	× ×	× ×	× ×
Subtotal = lb.	Subtotal = lb.	Subtotal = lb.	Subtotal = lb.	Subtotal = lb.	Subtotal = lb.

Exercise 5:   Total Weight _____ lb.   Time: _____ min.   Power Factor _____ lb./min.   Power Index _____

OVERALL WORKOUT:

Total Weight **7,300** lb.   Time: **21** min.   Power Factor **348** lb./min.   Power Index **2.5**
❾ ❸ ❿ ⓫

Exercise Subtotal = Weight × Reps × Sets   ■ Power Factor = lb./min.   ■ Power Index = Total Weight × Power Factor ÷ 1,000,000

3. Subtract your Start Time from your Finish Time to get the Total Time of your workout. Always express this in minutes only (for example, 95 minutes, not 1 hour and 35 minutes). Enter this at the top of the page and as the Total Time on the last line. The Total Time includes *all* the time used from the beginning of your workout (but not the warm-up) to the end. It includes rests between sets and rests between exercises and the time you took changing weights and getting a drink of water. It is *not* just the sum of your individual exercise times.

4. Calculate the total weight lifted per set by simple arithmetic. For example, if you perform 12 repetitions with 100 pounds, you multiply the two numbers to get 1,200 pounds. If you do 3 sets at that weight, you multiply by 3 to get 3,600 pounds. Put another way, you've lifted 100 pounds 36 times for a total weight lifted of 3,600 pounds. Do not include weight lifted during your warm-up. The warm-up itself should not degenerate into a workout. Instead utilize only the barest amount of energy and movement required to thoroughly warm up the joints, muscles, and connective tissues of the body parts you're going to be training, and perform only enough sets to obtain a slight pump and to achieve viscosity in the joints. For example, start out with just the empty bar you're about to utilize and perform 1 to 2 sets of fairly high (20 to 30) repetitions with it. Then add what for you is some appreciable resistance and perform 2 more sets of moderate reps (10 to 20). Add weight again and, if needed, perform 1 to 2 more sets. You should be adequately warmed up by this point and ready to start your real sets. For the sake of consistency, try to always use the same warm-up routine.

5. Calculate the Total Weight per exercise by adding the row of subtotal weights per set.

6. Measure the exercise Time from the time you start each individual exercise to the time you finish. Always include the time you rest in between sets. Do not include warm-up time. You will find a stopwatch very helpful for measuring this time.

7. Calculate the Power Factor by dividing the Total Weight by the time it took to lift it. So, if you lift 7,540 pounds in 18 minutes, your Power Factor is 419 pounds per minute (7,540 ÷ 18 = 419). This is the power output of your muscles. On average, every minute you lifted 419 pounds. If you can increase that number on your next workout, you will know that you have increased the overload and gained strength.

8. To calculate the Power Index, multiply the Total Weight by the Power Factor, then divide the product by 1,000,000. The significance of the Power Index is discussed below.

9. Calculate the Total Weight for the workout by adding the Total Weight from each exercise (in this example, 7,540 + 5,490 + 9,800 + 31,000 = 53,830 pounds). This number represents the total amount of weight you lifted during your workout.

10. To find the Power Factor for the Overall Workout, divide the Total Weight by the Total Time. In this case 53,830 ÷ 18 = 2,991.

11. To calculate the Power Index for your workout, multiply the Total Weight by the Power Factor and divide the product by 1,000,000. In this example, 53,830 × 2,991 ÷ 1,000,000 = 161.

The Power Factor measures the amount of weight lifted (in pounds) in the amount of time (in minutes) that it takes to do the lifting. The Power Factor is expressed in pounds per minute (lb./min.). It is elegantly simple yet profound in its result: it measures the muscular output of every exercise you perform! Now that we can quantify muscular output, the strength athlete can clearly compare the effectiveness of factors such as number of reps per set, number of sets per exercise, timing, weight, number of days off between workouts, and diet.

ENGINEERING YOUR NEXT WORKOUT

One of the most powerful aspects of Power Factor Training is that it allows you to plan a workout ahead of time in order to achieve a target goal and guarantee all-important progressive overload. The calculations necessary to do this are still fairly simple, and we encourage you to familiarize yourself with the technique, as it is the key to guaranteeing that every workout is effective, efficient, and progressive. Keep in mind that the two keys to maximum overload are total weight and time. Those are the only two factors that you will adjust in your workouts.

For example, suppose you bench-press a total weight lifted of 13,040 pounds and generate a Power Factor of 1,580 pounds/minute. Suppose you do this in 8.25 minutes. Now, you set a goal of achieving a 20 percent increase in your total weight and a 10 percent increase in your Power Factor the next time you perform the bench press. Simply follow these steps (on page 196):

1. Add 20 percent to 13,040 pounds (13,040 lb. × 1.20 = 15,650 lb.).
2. Add 10 percent to 1,580 pounds/minute (1,580 × 1.10 = 1,738 lb./min.).
3. Divide the goal total weight by the goal Power Factor to get the time allowed to perform the lifting (15,650 lb. ÷ 1,738 lb./min. = 9.0 min.).

After making these simple calculations, you know exactly what you have to do in your next workout to ensure that your muscular overload (that is, intensity) is higher: you have to lift 15,650 pounds in 9 minutes. You can achieve your goal total weight simply by adding an extra set, adding more reps to each set, or using a heavier weight so that the total will be 15,650 pounds As you work out, keep an eye on your stopwatch to ensure that you don't go over the 9 minutes you've set as your target time, and you will be certain that your Power Factor and Power Index have increased.

Here is one of the most important things to keep in mind. Ideally, no two workouts should ever be the same because each time you return to the gym you are a different man. If your last workout was properly engineered, it stimulated muscle growth. If you allowed yourself the required time for recovery and growth, you are a stronger person when you return to the gym. Therefore, performing the same workout as last time is useless. Since your muscles are now capable of more output, the old workout will not trigger any growth response. Get it? That's what progressive overload is all about. Do the same workout every time and you get nowhere; engineer an ever-increasing overload and you get steadily stronger. The engineering is done with the Power Factor and Power Index numbers.

You can set goals for one or all exercises you perform and for your complete workout as well. It is difficult to overstate the tremendous value of this ability to plan every workout to ensure that it is productive. This is the element of Power Factor Training that creates its efficiency and is the reason that such a high percentage of its trainees can work out once a week or less and still see consistent improvement all the way to the muscularity level that they desire. Every workout is a positive step toward the trainee's ultimate goal. Compare this to the old systems of everyone's following a prescribed chart of exercises for six weeks, then switching to another chart for six more weeks, and so on. Every trainee used the same daily schedule and repetition schemes, regardless of the fact that there is a huge amount of variation between individuals (remember the "sweet spot"?). Power Factor

Training gives you the ability to engineer every workout that you perform to be maximally productive for your particular physiology.

PROGRESS GRAPH

This technique of scientifically planning your goals and monitoring your results permits the highest possible muscular overload each workout and the greatest possible gains in size and strength. You will be able to see your chest and arms training progress by plotting your Power Factor and Power Index numbers on the Progress Graph. (You may photocopy these blank graphs for your personal use.) The trend that you should see on the graph is a consistent increase in your Power Factor and Power Index numbers on both individual exercises and your entire workout.

These graphs allow you enough room to plot four months of specialized training. This is more than enough for this type of

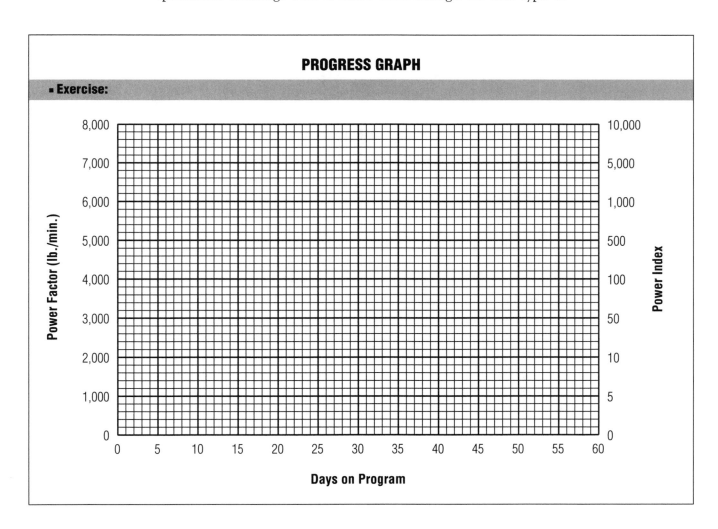

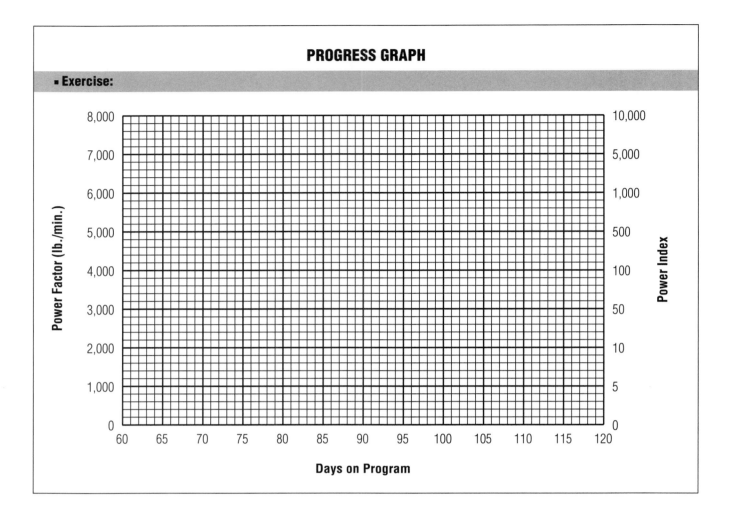

program. Even the most severely lagging chests and arms will be well caught up with the rest of your muscle groups long before four months have elapsed. In fact, six weeks of this training will probably make your chest and arms the two strongest areas of your body.

From time to time a workout may not yield an increase, and you may even see a decrease in your numbers. This, as you will discover, can be caused by a variety of circumstances. You may have worked out after eating too few complex carbohydrates, or after having had too little sleep, or when not being able to mentally concentrate due to stress. However, the number-one cause of a prolonged inability to improve is overtraining. It is critical to remember that muscular growth takes place only after you have recovered from your last workout, and the recovery and growth processes each require time to complete themselves. If you do not allow for this fact your muscles cannot grow.

Let's examine one subject's change in Power Index during a period of twenty workouts over sixty days.

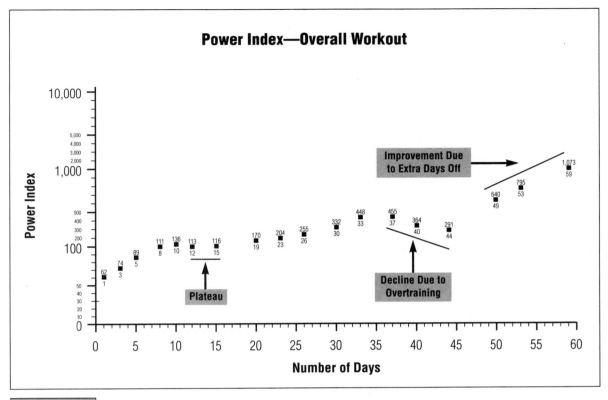

KEY

136 → Power Index

10 → Days on Program

As you can see, progress was steady on a Monday-Wednesday-Friday schedule, but by the twelfth day the Power Index declined. By switching to a two-days-per-week schedule, the trainee gave his metabolism the required time not only to recover but to increase its muscle mass. On a twice-a-week schedule tremendous gains were made up to the thirty-third day. At this point, rather than just hitting a plateau, his muscular output sharply decreased. Once again, he corrected this by adding more time off between workouts. As expected, his Power Index again showed a tremendous improvement.

Note that the change in Power Index from Day 1 to Day 59 is enormous. This reflects a great increase in both the total amount of weight lifted and the rate of lifting (pounds/minute). Such numerical gains can be achieved only through a great increase in muscular strength and therefore create a corresponding increase in muscular size. Using Power Factor Training, an athlete can quickly and graphically identify and correct even subtle changes in his performance through proper alterations in the workout and/or the training schedule. Power Factor Training identifies and prevents the chronic plateaus and overtraining that plague strength athletes who rely on the crude gauge of feel and instinct to measure their performance.

UNDERSTANDING RECOVERY

Like all other physical characteristics of humans, recovery ability after exercise varies very widely between individuals. After identical workouts, one person may be able to return to the gym in forty-eight hours and see an increase in his Power Factor and Power Index, while another person may need a full week in order to both recover sufficiently and show improvement.

When you use Power Factor Training you have the ability to see how well you have recovered by virtue of your Power Factor and Power Index numbers. If you return to the gym too soon after a workout, you will not perform as well and your numbers will reflect this. When this happens, just add a day or two of recovery until your numbers show some improvement.

During the development of Power Factor Training it became necessary, for a variety of reasons, for both of us authors to take six weeks off from working out. When we finally returned to the gym we were mentally prepared for a light workout. To our surprise, we discovered that as the workout progressed, not only did we have no sign of atrophy but our strength had taken a quantum leap upward. In fact, we both set new personal records in every exercise we performed.

It is clear that recovery can be measured along a range of time that begins with the first day you can return to the gym and expect an improvement and ends with the last day you can return to the gym and expect an improvement. Power Factor Training will allow you to precisely determine your personal range of recovery. Depending on a variety of personal factors, your own range may be anywhere from two or three days to many weeks.

Consequently, if you are the sort of person who loves to train, that is, who wants to be in the gym as frequently as possible, you can work at the close end of your range of recovery by returning to the gym as soon as you are able. If, on the other hand, you have commitments or an otherwise busy schedule, you can work out less frequently by working at the far end of your recovery range. You won't lose ground in your Power Factor and Power Index numbers. In either case, you'll make dramatic and consistent progress.

The Recovery Time Spectrum

The value of knowing your personal range of recovery ability is that you'll know with mathematical precision exactly when you honestly do have to train and when you don't. Just because somebody else can train three days a week and make progress is irrelevant in your personal training considerations; he may have stumbled onto a margin of training that falls within his range of personal recovery ability. The problem will arise when he eventually ceases to make progress. He won't know if his lack of progress is due to having reached the upper limits of his genetic potential, having become stale, or training with insufficient intensity to continue the growth process.

On the other hand, if you know how many days it takes you to recover from having lifted X number of pounds in a given workout, then it stands to reason that it will take even more days to recover once you've increased your Power Factor. No longer do you need to feel guilty because you didn't train one day last week. You would have been doing more harm than good to your strength and physique aspirations if you worked out even one day sooner than the first day that your recovery ability had replenished itself.

What we've learned about recovery ability is that there exists a general and very limited supply, almost like a small reservoir. Every time you lift a weight, you dip into this reservoir a certain percentage, a percentage that must be replaced before the growth process can occur. In fact, some exercise physiologists have theorized that while the average trainee has the potential to increase his starting level of strength some 300 percent within the first year of training, his ability to recover from such workouts increases by only 50 percent. This creates a fundamental challenge to the trainee, as his rate of overloading his system increases at a different rate than his ability to recover from the overload. Think of it this way: say that your body has the ability to recover from 100 "units" of exercise per day. When you start your training, your strength is minimal and you may be capable of generating only 70 or 80 units of overload. No problem; your metabolic system can recover from that in one day. As you grow stronger, however, your muscles have the ability to generate 150 units of overload, which will take two days to recover from. By the time your recovery ability begins to improve, your muscular output might be up to 300 to 350 units of overload and you must take multiple days off between workouts. This is a critical balance, as the trainee who returns to the gym too soon will have a recovery deficit that has not been paid off in sufficient recovery "units" and will just dig himself a bigger hole from which to recuperate.

Moreover, if you are the sort of person who has a lagging body part (and that's quite likely since you bought this book), you could have certain muscles that require more recovery time than others do. So even though your central nervous system could support some more muscle growth in your legs, for example, your triceps may still be too depleted to perform a productive arm workout. Power Factor Training allows you to identify whether or not your triceps have recovered sufficiently. That's a real boon to specialized training.

In Chapter 10 we will answer all of the most common questions that we have received over the years. As it stands, you now have everything you need to ensure the highest level of success in your chest and arm training. Using the information and techniques in this book, you will be able to garner the fastest and greatest possible increases in muscle size and strength.

Now, get busy.

BLANK PERFORMANCE RECORD AND EXERCISE PERFORMANCE RECORD

The blank forms that follow may be photocopied for your personal use.

WORKOUT RECORD   Date: ____ / ____ / ____

Start Time: _____   **Finish Time:** _____   **Total Time:** _____

■ Exercise:

Weight Reps Sets	Weight Reps Sets	Weight Reps Sets	Weight Reps Sets	Weight Reps Sets	Weight Reps Sets
× ×	× ×	× ×	× ×	× ×	× ×
Subtotal = lb.	Subtotal = lb.	Subtotal = lb.	Subtotal = lb.	Subtotal = lb.	Subtotal = lb.

Exercise 1:   *Total Weight* _____ *lb.*   *Time:* _____ *min.*   *Power Factor* _____ *lb./min.*   *Power Index* _____

■ Exercise:

Weight Reps Sets	Weight Reps Sets	Weight Reps Sets	Weight Reps Sets	Weight Reps Sets	Weight Reps Sets
× ×	× ×	× ×	× ×	× ×	× ×
Subtotal = lb.	Subtotal = lb.	Subtotal = lb.	Subtotal = lb.	Subtotal = lb.	Subtotal = lb.

Exercise 2:   *Total Weight* _____ *lb.*   *Time:* _____ *min.*   *Power Factor* _____ *lb./min.*   *Power Index* _____

■ Exercise:

Weight Reps Sets	Weight Reps Sets	Weight Reps Sets	Weight Reps Sets	Weight Reps Sets	Weight Reps Sets
× ×	× ×	× ×	× ×	× ×	× ×
Subtotal = lb.	Subtotal = lb.	Subtotal = lb.	Subtotal = lb.	Subtotal = lb.	Subtotal = lb.

Exercise 3:   *Total Weight* _____ *lb.*   *Time:* _____ *min.*   *Power Factor* _____ *lb./min.*   *Power Index* _____

■ Exercise:

Weight Reps Sets	Weight Reps Sets	Weight Reps Sets	Weight Reps Sets	Weight Reps Sets	Weight Reps Sets
× ×	× ×	× ×	× ×	× ×	× ×
Subtotal = lb.	Subtotal = lb.	Subtotal = lb.	Subtotal = lb.	Subtotal = lb.	Subtotal = lb.

Exercise 4:   *Total Weight* _____ *lb.*   *Time:* _____ *min.*   *Power Factor* _____ *lb./min.*   *Power Index* _____

■ Exercise:

Weight Reps Sets	Weight Reps Sets	Weight Reps Sets	Weight Reps Sets	Weight Reps Sets	Weight Reps Sets
× ×	× ×	× ×	× ×	× ×	× ×
Subtotal = lb.	Subtotal = lb.	Subtotal = lb.	Subtotal = lb.	Subtotal = lb.	Subtotal = lb.

Exercise 5:   *Total Weight* _____ *lb.*   *Time:* _____ *min.*   *Power Factor* _____ *lb./min.*   *Power Index* _____

OVERALL WORKOUT:

Total Weight _____ *lb.*   *Time:* _____ *min.*   *Power Factor* _____ *lb./min.*   *Power Index* _____

Exercise Subtotal = Weight × Reps × Sets   ■   *Power Factor = lb./min.*   ■   *Power Index = Total Weight × Power Factor ÷ 1,000,000*

EXERCISE/WORKOUT PERFORMANCE RECORD

■ **Exercise:**

Date	Total Weight	% Change	Power Factor	% Change	Power Index	+ or − Change

10

Questions and Answers

Number-One Mistake

Q. What is the number-one mistake made by people using Power Factor Training?

A. They don't keep track of their Power Factor and Power Index numbers. Many people give our system a quick read and determine it's *all* about doing strong-range exercises. Then they proceed to overtrain with strong-range exercises instead of over-training with full-range exercises the way they always had. The Power Factor and Power Index were invented to measure intensity. Once there was a measurement, it was easy to identify the superior value of strong-range partials. But, it is necessary to keep using the numbers in order to ensure progressive overload and avoid the plateaus and overtraining that are certain to occur with fixed-frequency training schedules. The numbers, in fact, are the exact indicators of when to alter training frequency.

Number-Two Mistake

Q. What is the number-two mistake people make using Power Factor Training?

A. They choose weights that are too light. In every case where we have supervised a workout, the trainee is oblivious to how much strength he has in his strongest range. For example, we (the authors) perform strong-range bench presses in the 600-pound range. It is very common for leg press weights to approach or exceed 2,000 pounds in very strong men. Despite these facts, we still get the occasional letter from someone who says, "I could full-range bench 200 pounds. After two months of Power Factor Training I worked up to 300-pound reps, but when I checked my full-range bench press it was still just 200. Power Factor Training didn't work for me." The truth is he didn't work for it. If a person can full-range bench 200, he should be doing reps with 300 on Day 1. In two months he should be in the 500- to 600-pound range. That stimulates enormous growth!

Number-Three Mistake
Q. What is the number-three mistake people make?

A. They work out too often or augment their training with other workouts. This is a tough one to get across to people. Rest is very important! These workouts are extremely intense. The *only* way you can maintain this intensity is to do no other strength training whatsoever on your off days.

Remember, we have tested all of these parameters. We tried working people more times a week; it reduced results. We tried more exercises; it reduced results. We tried mixing full- and partial-range exercises; it reduced results. It's all about the Intensity vs. Duration of Muscular Output graph back in Chapter 2; we have learned that *nothing* is more important than intensity! That is what you are measuring with your Power Factor and Power Index numbers. Sacrifice intensity in favor of anything and you will reduce your results.

Mixed Results
Q. After steady progress, this week my numbers went up on my arm workout but not on my chest workout. What should I do?

A. We have learned that different muscle groups require different amounts of localized recovery. Localized recovery requirements are a little different than the systemic recovery requirements, which when ignored can cause a lack of progress in every part of the body. Even when other muscles are progressing, skip the muscle group that shows little or no progress. In other words, if you have been training your chest once per week and this week you showed no progress, don't train your chest again until two weeks from now. This extra time off will allow the affected muscles to fully recover and even grow. You'll know they've grown when you see the numbers increase again.

Where is the strongest range?

Q. I want to do some experimentation with other exercises but on some exercises, for example, leg extensions, leg curls, and bent-over rows, I'm not sure what part of the range of motion involves full contraction.

A. It's always heartening to find out that people are willing to experiment with new applications to their training. Remember the objective of any exercise should be to provide maximum overload to the muscle or muscle group that the exercise targets. By definition, maximum overload will be achieved in the range of motion that permits you to handle the heaviest weight possible for that exercise. This is easy to see in exercises like dips used to overload triceps. From a fully locked out position the point of maximum triceps overload will be out of lockout and down only an inch or two, rather than at the point where your body is fully lowered and your hands are near your armpits. The same is true on a close-grip bench press, where the strongest range is the last few inches of reach. The issue is a little more confused on an exercise like the lat pulldown. It can be argued that maximum contraction in a lat pulldown occurs when the bar is pulled all the way to your chest. But the problem is that in this position your elbows are also bent and your biceps are performing a significant amount of work to hold that position in that range. As your biceps weaken, your elbows are forced to straighten and allow the bar to rise toward the end of your reach. However, during the first one to three inches of motion in the lat pulldown, the biceps perform virtually none of the work of lowering the bar. Moving the weight in this part of the range will produce a fatigue in the lats that has to be felt to be believed. We have always seen the best progress in lat development when using this range. When experimenting with any new exercise, just remember maximum overload will occur when you are in a position that allows the maximum weight to be used.

Super-Slow Reps

Q. What are your thoughts on super-slow reps?

A. Utilizing super-slow reps (a technique that has been variously described as taking 10 to 15 seconds per rep to 1 minute or more per rep) is a method that will stimulate muscle growth. The drawbacks of the technique are (1) if there is a full range of motion involved, then a lighter weight must be used in order for it to be manageable in the weakest range, and (2) whenever a weight is being lowered, you can never be sure how hard you are pressing against that weight. For example, when a bar weighs 200 pounds and you are lowering it (super slow or otherwise) all we know for certain is that you are not pressing up with 200 pounds of force. You may be pressing up with 199 pounds or with 170 pounds. In effect, lowering a weight gives you some amount of rest. So comparisons of intensity from workout to workout begin to get vague. That's not good.

Both Power Factor Training and our static contraction research study prove that significant gains in mass and strength can be achieved without ever operating in the weakest range of motion. We suspect that the greatest benefits achieved while performing super-slow sets is garnered when the weight is held in the strongest range.

How Power Factor Training Builds Muscular Mass

Q. I'm very interested in the mechanics of muscle growth. I understand that it is the increased work per unit of time that is the stimulus for hypertrophy (muscle growth) to occur. But I'm wondering what some of the changes are that take place within, say, the biceps muscle that result in its getting larger as a result of Power Factor Training?

A. Power Factor Training places a phenomenal demand on the body's ability to supply energy to muscles. To use your example, the body stores energy within the biceps muscle's cells in the form of glycogen, and the amount of glycogen, more or less, determines the ability of the biceps or any other muscle to continue contracting. Conversely, when the biceps muscle's glycogen supply is fully exhausted, contraction ceases. Exhausting these stores of glycogen, however, causes the body to adapt by increasing the capacity to store extra glycogen in the biceps muscle. In fact, bodybuilders may possess twice the glycogen supply of nontraining individuals. It follows from this that if more glycogen is available, the ability to train hard for longer periods (a requisite for stimulating muscle growth) is thereby increased, along with your Power Factor numbers. Increased glycogen storage in the muscles also causes them to become bigger—a fact that explains why bodybuilding competitors often "carb up" before a contest. Another mass-building effect of Power Factor Training is an increase in blood volume in the area being trained. The higher volume of blood directed toward the biceps would help to create more capillaries in the area, which would receive more oxygen and thereby increase that muscle group's size potential. It's been further established that Power Factor Training can increase the natural production of growth hormone; the greater the overload or work per unit of time during the period of contraction, the greater the degree of stimulation of this naturally occurring anabolic. Finally, Power Factor Training allows you to use the heaviest weights possible to stimulate mass increases, and a muscle's force is directly proportionate to its cross-sectional area. Simply stated, this means that a stronger muscle is a bigger muscle.

Sets and Reps

Q. What is the ideal number of sets and reps I should be performing in Power Factor Training?

A. The answer to this question is going to vary with each individual who is using Power Factor Training. You could start out by performing only 4 to 6 sets of an exercise and 10 to 30 repetitions, then look at your Power Factor numbers. Adjust the weight, sets, and reps so that your Power Factor numbers are constantly going up. We've found that you will generally stimulate more growth if you try to perform a lot of repetitions with a moderate to heavy weight, as your "work in a unit of time" will have increased.

Q. I've heard the formula prescribed in most gyms: if you want to build mass, you have to perform only 6 to 8 reps with heavy weights. Is this formula scientifically invalid?

A. It's invalid for most people because there exists a highly individual relationship between the amount of weight that you are capable of lifting, the number of repetitions you can perform with it, and the time that it takes you to do it. This is what creates your Power Factor. The Power Factor is going to vary for each individual.

Tracking two of these three factors results in bell curves. On the first bell curve, for the amount of weight you can lift (that is, if you can lift only a small amount of weight) you're going to be at the low end of the bell curve and your Power Factor is going to be low. If you are able to perform your set with an extremely heavy weight, you may find that you are capable of lifting it so few times that you're going to be on the low end of the opposite side of the bell curve and your Power Factor will still be low. Now let's look at the bell curve for the number of repetitions you perform. If you do only one repetition, it's going to be very hard to get a high Power Factor. At the opposite end of that bell curve is 200 repetitions or 300 repetitions. A weight that you can do 200 repetitions with is going to be a very light weight. Again, because of the light weight multiplied by the high repetitions, you're still going to have a low Power Factor. You need to find that middle ground or "sweet spot" on both of those bell curves. There the optimum weight and the right number of repetitions will be somewhere in the middle of the bell curves. These amounts will be different from person to person because of innate genetic differences. So, while performing 6 to 8 repetitions may be right for a certain percentage of the population (perhaps 5 percent), for other people it's going to need to be higher or lower, although it's hard to imagine lower reps than that. For most people, the "sweet spot" is going to involve high repetitions with a moderate to heavy weight.

How Heavy?

Q. So while heavy weights are important to recruit and stimulate muscle fibers into growth, super-heavy weights aren't necessarily the key?

A. Heavy weights are important. In fact, that's why strong-range training is so effective: it allows your muscles to contract against much heavier resistance than they would be capable of in their weakest range while performing many repetitions. This results in a huge output of work in a unit of time—the formula for muscle growth. The problem with using a super-heavy weight, say, a 100 percent max, whether in your weakest range or strongest range, is that it's essentially a one-rep shot, which results in a very low Power Factor. For that one rep, you may well be recruiting as many muscle fibers as possible to move that weight. But once those fibers are fired, that's it. That's the end of the fiber output because you can't do a second rep with it. As a result, your Power Factor, or pounds per minute (your actual muscular output), is down, but your objective is always to try to get that up. Although a lot of fibers are stimulated with a one-rep effort, it's not as many as it would be if you performed multiple reps with a Power Factor of 2,000 pounds per minute. Say it takes you 4 seconds to raise your one-rep maximum. In those 4 seconds only would there be a high Power Factor. Looking at this from the point of view of physics, developing a high Power Factor for 4 seconds is not going to require the same overall power output as, say, a 50 percent lower initial Power Factor that is extended 500 percent longer or 1000 percent longer. Again, the key to muscle-growth stimulation is the amount of work done. Lifting a moderately heavy weight many times represents a lot more work than lifting a very heavy weight one time. This is the difference between alpha strength and beta strength.

Muscle Mass

Q. Does that increased work necessarily mean increased muscle mass?

A. It has to. Your muscles can do more work only by calling on the muscle fibers themselves to do more work—and there is a metabolic cost to that. You can probably get gains by going into the gym and doing a one-rep max for each exercise. But you don't get the gains on the same order as if you really pounded away doing rep after rep with a high Power Factor for multiple sets. With such a prolonged period of a high rate of muscular output, you'd really kick in that systemic overload. Again, the key to efficient strength training is to find that perfect relationship among weight, repetitions, and time. You'll get results if you screw up and you have too few reps and too heavy a weight, or too low a weight and too low reps. You'll even get an adaptive response if you work out at 70 percent efficiency—you'll get 70 percent of the growth you could have gotten. If you're at 40 percent efficiency, you'll get 40 percent of the growth you could have gotten. And, if you're training at 100 percent efficiency, then you'll receive 100 percent of the growth you could have. If you train with an eye toward achieving the absolute highest work per unit of time that you are capable of, then you will have stimulated the absolute most muscle growth you could possibly have stimulated. At this point, it is imperative that you stay out of the gym as long as necessary to recover and wait for the growth that you stimulated through your efforts in the gym to manifest. Then, when you come back to the gym, it's time to crunch your Power Factor numbers again, because now there's another spot on the bell curve that you're going to have to hit this time out to maximize your results. If you come back and do the same workout, it won't be enough this time, because you will have grown stronger.

Recovery

Q. Are you saying that with Power Factor Training, I should be training less frequently than three days per week?

A. We're saying that only your Power Factor numbers can reveal this answer. Most individuals look at recovery as something that takes place in a matter of days—one or two of them, three at the most. But our research now shows that full recovery from an intense workout may not occur for weeks. Exercise physiologists are now of the opinion that training produces a tremendous strain on the body's recuperative systems and that growth and strength increases don't occur until those systems have been allowed to work. Our own research and experiments with Power Factor Training show that working out three times a week (or more) is invariably counterproductive. In fact, even for beginners, training twice or once a week is far better. We're not talking about full-body workouts, either, but split routines working chest, back, and legs one day, for example, followed by shoulders and arms several days after that. However, even if you train each body part just once a week, you may not be giving your body enough time to fully recover. If you're not gaining strength every time out (and by looking at your Power Factor numbers you'll know how to measure this on a workout-by-workout basis so there's never any ambiguity), you may want to take even more time off between workouts. You can go as long as six weeks between workouts and still gain size and strength. We realize that certain members of the bodybuilding culture simply like to spend a lot of time in the gym even though they don't really have to (as parents, we're both happy spending as little time in the gym as we can). These individuals now have a means of measuring what day is the soonest that they can return to the gym and have another productive workout. In addition (and particularly for these people), it is important to remember that there are many things you can do in a health club besides lift weights, such as cardiovascular or flexibility training, both of which are crucial to overall fitness.

Full Range Equals Reduced Results

Q. *Would you be recruiting an equal number of muscle fibers if you put the weight at a place where physiologically it's at a disadvantage, where the angle of lifting is such that it seems harder to your muscles to lift—even if it's a full-range exercise?*

A. Simply because something seems harder does not make it productive. Here's an example. You could deliberately execute a muscle contraction while you are at a mechanical disadvantage, say, perform a dumbbell curl with your arm behind your back. That is only going to result in your using less weight, which in turn will result in your work performed in a given unit of time dropping way off. The testing of the exercises that we've reported on in this book were all done through a full range of motion for the sake of familiarity. Everyone is familiar with full-range exercise. From this data, we learned that some exercises were very low in terms of efficiency, for allowing the trainee to generate a high work per unit of time output. Others were higher. If you performed the exercises that we discovered to be the most effective in their strongest range exclusively, the weight your muscles would be contracting against and the amount of repetitions you could perform with it would be much higher, greatly increasing the work-per-unit-of-time output of your muscles. If your muscles have the work-per-unit-of-time potential to perform 20 repetitions on the bench press with 400 pounds, of what benefit would being at a mechanical disadvantage be? Why reduce that output to 20 reps with 100 pounds? Growth is stimulated only by increasing the amount of work your muscles must perform in a given unit of time; this means you must constantly increase the weight, not look for ways to make lighter weights feel heavier. This is the problem with exercising in a full range of motion: your muscles are always forced to contract against a resistance that is at most half of what they are capable of contracting against—and 50 percent output results in only half of the stimulation you could be receiving.

Hitting the Chest from Different Angles

Q. I have always been told that if you really want to train a body part then you need to train it with at least three different exercises. You can't, for example, just do decline barbell bench presses for your lower pecs because you also need to do incline bench presses to stimulate the upper region of the pectoral muscles, and you need to do dumbbell flies to get the outer regions of the chest. And, when I come out of the gym after a workout like this, I know I've done something productive because all these regions of my chest are very sore. Are you saying that this soreness—and those exercises—don't mean anything?

A. What you're talking about is a perceived level of stimulation as evidenced by postworkout soreness caused by the pain receptors within your chest. What we're concerned with is not pain receptors but muscle stimulation. And they are two completely different things. To use your example of training the chest, the fibers in the pectoral region are activated by how heavy the weight is that you're calling upon them to move and by the effective work you are making them perform over a given unit of time. The greater the muscular output (weight + work ÷ time), the more fibers are brought into play. Now, by definition, these exercises that we've established as having low Power Factors are necessarily ones that limit fiber stimulation to one region of the pectoral region. So, you're in effect deliberately employing ineffective exercises in the training of your chest (that is, exercises that limit—rather than maximize fiber involvement). It's the equivalent of saying, "I want to employ three inefficient exercises to take the place of the one efficient exercise." Why would anyone choose to do this? There is actually very little evidence to support the contention that it is possible to completely isolate particular regions of the pectoral complex owing to the fact that the chest muscles are served by the same tendon of insertion, which means that both the upper and lower pecs are stimulated every time the impulse is sent for contraction in the chest region. The bench press, particularly if performed in your strongest range, provides sufficient stimulation to the bulk of—if not all of—your available chest fibers. And even if it was only 95 percent efficient, the difference that would make in the appearance of your physique would be imperceptible. We've yet to encounter anybody who can tell at a glance who performs three exercises for their chest and who performs only one, or who trains with machines and who trains with free weights. And the reason is because muscle growth is dependent solely upon your muscles' performing more work in a given unit of time. It doesn't make any difference to your physiology whether this increase of work in unit of time you're making your muscles perform comes from lifting a bucket of rocks, lifting a barbell, or training on a Nautilus machine. It's how much force is required to be generated to move that resistance. The greater the muscular output in a given unit of time, the greater the growth stimulation. And since the whole goal is a great amount of work in a unit of time, you're naturally going to gravitate toward those heavy compound exercises where you can lift the most you possibly can.

Take the leg press for your quads. This is an exercise in which you can simply pile on much more weight, and that allows you to lift more weight in a given unit of time. If you pick some other exercise for the legs, it's only going to give you a lower Power Factor. The entire science aside, doesn't it seem self-evident that there must be muscle fibers that aren't getting taxed? Say you have the capability to lift 4,800 pounds per minute, but then you go and select three exercises where you're limited to 500, 1,400, and 1,800 pounds per minute, such as barbell pullovers, Nautilus machine pullovers, and dumbbell flies. It should be evident that those are innately inferior exercises. They're taxing small amounts of muscle fibers compared to other exercises such as barbell bench presses. And, again, that's the physics of exercise: the motor you need to do that amount of work in a unit of time is a bigger motor. And the muscle you need to do that amount of work in a unit of time is a bigger muscle. The fact that these other exercises limit, rather than enhance, muscle fiber involvement is a reason to stay away from them.

Forced Repetitions

Q. What about including forced repetitions after reaching a state of muscular failure in a set? Will this stimulate additional muscle growth?

A. When you think about it, what is a forced repetition? Having a training partner help you lift the bar to complete several additional repetitions of an exercise is simply a means of increasing the amount of work your muscles are doing in that unit of time (which *is* good, but not as efficient as training solely in your strongest range). And at that, given that you seldom perform more than four or five forced reps in any given set, you should probably simply put the weight down, take a brief rest, and then perform another set of higher repetitions. Incidentally, people typically go to failure only in full- or weak-range exercise. A bodybuilder might fail at the bottom or weakest position in the range of motion and then have a partner help him out of his weakest range into his strongest range. And it is in this range that he is able to take over and complete the repetition. Here, again, is the argument in favor of strong-range repetitions. The bodybuilder has hit complete failure; he can't lift the weight even one inch further. But in his strongest range he still has lots of muscle fiber strength left, which remains untapped. And the whole idea of progressive overload is to lift a little more today than you did during your last workout. This is why it's so much more beneficial to engage in that progressive overload in the strongest range instead of down in the weakest range. In the weak range you are not taxing all of the fibers, because the weight employed is too light and you're hitting failure prematurely.

Productive Reps

Q. A very well-known bodybuilder who espouses the scientific, high-intensity method of training has said that the most productive rep of, say, an eight-rep set is the last one because that is the repetition that requires a maximum effort to complete. It's this last rep that requires an all-out effort to move that weight, and this causes your body to dip into its reserves and overcompensate with increased muscle mass. He says anything more than the least amount of exercise required to stimulate growth, which in this case is one full-range set, amounts to overtraining. What are your thoughts on this?

A. Our position is that if he recommends employing full-range repetitions his logic isn't extending far enough. At the end of a full-range set of barbell curls done to failure, the trainee is still capable of performing repetitions in his strongest range. When the trainee hits failure at the end of this point, which rep of this set is the most productive: the rep where the trainee can no longer lift the weight the sixteen inches or so required to complete a full-range repetition, or the repetition where the trainee can no longer move the resistance even a quarter of an inch? What we advocate is the abandonment of full-range training altogether. We agree that anything more than the least amount of stimulation required is overtraining and that the stimulation required is an increase in the work your muscles are made to perform in a given unit of time. But it doesn't follow that employing an inferior amount of stimulation will lead to maximum muscle growth. Again, if you are training in your strongest range, your muscles will be working at their full potential and your muscular adaptation will be immediate and dramatic.

Eating Bread

Q. *You mentioned in your book* Power Factor Training *that for people seeking to lose bodyfat, the important thing is to reduce their calorie intake below their maintenance levels and that it's all right for a person to eat anything he wants. Does this hold true for eating a high-carbohydrate food such as bread?*

A. Yes. As long as your total calorie intake is reduced, you'll lose fat. There is nothing fattening about bread, per se, as a slice of bread contains only 75 calories. Contrary to the maxim that it's not the bread that is fattening; it's what you put on it, there is nothing fattening even about what you put on it. It is the total number of calories consumed above your personal maintenance amount throughout the course of a day or accumulatively throughout a week, month, or year, that results in the acquisition and/or expansion of adipose tissue. Bread, jams, peanut butter, margarine, and so on are not themselves going to cause you to become fat. If you ate your maintenance amount of calories and then consumed bread and/or preserves additionally, then the calories contained in that bread and preserves could prove to be the proverbial straw that broke the camel's back, causing you to gain some bodyfat. However, even then you would have to eat twenty-five slices of bread and thirteen tablespoons of peanut butter over and above your daily maintenance to gain one pound of fat—a considerable undertaking in its own right. So bread is quite safe to consume while dieting. In fact, Michigan State University published the results of a nutritional study that revealed that college students who were allowed to eat whatever they wanted—provided they ate twelve slices of high-fiber bread each day—lost weight. This was owing to the fact that the bread was filling, which reduced their desire for additional food, and was comparatively low in calories, which would account for the weight loss. Truly food for thought. *Bon appétit.*

Weight-Lifting Belts

Q. Do I need a weight belt or not? I have just recently started training and noticed that while some bodybuilders wear them, others never do. Are they a necessity or simply a custom?

A. Your query is a common one, and the answer is quite simple, although dependent solely upon your choice of exercises. If you are routinely engaged in exercises that are, from a kinesiological standpoint, potentially or actually stressful to your vertebrae, then yes, you should wear a lifting belt. Ideally, you should substitute the potentially dangerous exercises for ones that are less risky, but if you feel that you must continue to use such exercises, then a weight or support belt is definitely a wise acquisition. Exercises such as standing presses, deadlifts, squats, and barbell and particularly T-bar rowing put a tremendous volume of pressure not only on your erector spinae muscles but on your spine as well. And while a lifting belt does not prevent pressure from being directed toward your lower back, it does aid in the dissipation and distribution of the pressure, which will definitely prolong your training life and stave off the possibility of injury. Belts are, interestingly enough, required only for free-weight movements, as machines such as Nautilus, Universal, and Kaiser are designed and manufactured to eliminate the mechanical drawbacks of free weights. Your observation that some bodybuilders do wear belts while others don't is quite valid. Some wear them for legitimate reasons, such as doing heavy powerlifts, with which they need all of the support and protection that they can get. Others, however, are more poseur than serious bodybuilder. They wear lifting belts usually with unnecessarily torn T-shirts, lifting gloves (now there's a real necessity), and of course the obligatory leather straps (for "support purposes," of course!). Then, all decked out in this gear in which they resemble a cross between Marlon Brando in *The Wild One* and a knight from the Middle Ages, they walk over to a moderately weighted barbell, draw and expel several loud breaths, and proceed to throw the weight up and down in an attempt to perform a set of barbell curls while screaming like a banshee. This is, of course, palpable nonsense to those who know anything about the requisites of productive exercise, and it is needlessly intimidating to those who are newcomers to the science. In other words, if you are going to seriously perform a heavy set of standing presses, barbell or T-bar rows, deadlifts, or squats, or if you presently experience back problems, then a belt would be a useful item to have among your training paraphernalia. If, however, you're thinking of purchasing a belt because other people are wearing them, then stop now before you digress to the point where you become one of the attention-seeking masters of interruption just described. Look for reasons why you should or should not obtain or pursue something, not convention. In the quest for training truth there can exist no sacred cows. Tradition, convention, imitation, or custom have no place in the training concepts of the modern bodybuilder. Only facts should sway or anchor your beliefs, your conclusions, and ultimately your actions. This is true regarding not only your training but all other aspects of your life as well.

Exercises to Lengthen a Muscle

Q. Is it possible, as some bodybuilders claim, to actually lengthen a muscle by performing exercises that excessively stretch it? For example, can performing Scott curls extend a short biceps? If so, how do I do this?

A. To our knowledge, it is not possible to lengthen muscles to any appreciable degree by stretching them. As our muscles are attached to our bones via tendons, the only way that they could be lengthened would be if you had your tendons surgically cut and then reattached further down the bone. Such a procedure is neither pleasurable nor practical. While Scott or preacher bench curls do serve to stretch or hyperextend the biceps muscle, they do little or anything to alter the length of this muscle group. For example, witness the biceps of former Mr. Olympia winners Chris Dickerson and Franco Columbu. These are men who performed preacher curls frequently and intensively over the course of their competitive bodybuilding careers, yet never acquired the long, full biceps of the exercise's namesake, Larry Scott. Instead the biceps of both remained short though impressive. Muscle length is a genetic trait and, as such, is not subject to alteration shy of surgery. Don't worry about the fact that your biceps are not as full as some champion's, because these traits are genetically predetermined. Just as we can't all be over six feet tall and have faces like Tom Selleck's, neither can we all be so genetically gifted to build physiques like Arnold Schwarzenegger. Simply train hard and develop yourself to the best of your abilities, because you cannot accurately compare yourself or your achievements to anybody but yourself. And similarly, owing to innate physiological differences, nobody else (including bodybuilding champions) can accurately compare with you. You're unique, and it is always infinitely more desirable to cultivate your own specific individuality to its fullest potential rather than to simply copy someone else. Who knows? Your genetic potential, once realized through intelligent training and dietary principles, may far exceed that of the champions that you envy—but you'll never realize your potential unless you try.

Definition Exercises

Q. I have been bodybuilding for several years now and have made considerable gains in size and strength. It has struck me that perhaps at this stage of my training it would be wise for me to become ripped. But I still want to hold on to my existing size. What are the best definition exercises for the different body parts in your opinion?

A. We should begin our reply to your query by stating immediately that there is no such thing as a definition exercise. *Definition*, per se, is strictly a matter of shedding enough fat from under the skin in order to allow the muscle that you've developed to stand out in bold relief. As definition is exclusively a matter of losing fat, it is solely achieved via diet (that is, by taking in fewer calories than you expend) and by your voluntary activity levels. While it is true that you will lose fat quicker by markedly increasing your activity levels, the difference is not all that significant. Conversely, even by fasting, you would be hard-pressed to lose more than five or six ounces of fat per day. While there is no such thing as a definition exercise, specific exercises do exist that require more energy/calories (the excess of which is responsible for fat storage) and thus help in developing a more defined appearance. Many in the field of bodybuilding will say, for example, that seated leg extensions are a definition exercise whereas heavy barbell squats are a mass exercise. But this, is a distinction without meaning. As a matter of fact, barbell squats would probably be a better exercise for acquiring definition than would leg extensions simply because they are the most demanding in terms of energy (that is, calorie) expenditure. The secret then to obtaining a more defined or "ripped" appearance is to follow a calorie-reduced diet and select exercises that demand the most energy to perform, such as squats, leg presses, and other heavy compound movements. In this way, not only do you burn more calories but your bigger and stronger muscles will burn more calories even while resting in order to sustain their existence, as larger muscles require and expend more calories at rest than does fat tissue. Consequently, a high rate of work in your training (work per unit of time) married to a reduced-calorie diet gives you a double dividend in the war against the definition-obscuring demon of adiposity.

Cheating
Q. I notice that a lot of bodybuilders who train full range have a tendency to cheat on exercises such as bench presses and standing barbell curls. Isn't this dangerous?

Arching your back when performing barbell bench presses is bad form that can lead to serious injury.

Arching your upper body during standing barbell curls places excessive strain on your spine.

A. Not only is this dangerous, but it's completely unnecessary. Cheating only occurs when a trainee attempts to hoist the resistance through a "sticking point." And since sticking points only occur in the weakest range of motion—a range that it is unnecessary to train in—it's a risk that needn't be taken. People who train full range have a tendency to want to impress whoever happens to be within a hundred yards of them, so they often select weights that they think will impress people as opposed to weights that will thoroughly stimulate the muscles to get bigger and stronger—the reason that they joined the gym in the first place. Remember that once a force other than that of muscular contraction is made to do the work, the targeted muscle group loses virtually any stimulation it may have been receiving. The light weights employed in full range involve the barest minimum of muscle fibers required to move the resistance. Your objective as a bodybuilder is to involve as many fibers as possible in order to ensure maximum muscle stimulation and thereby broaden your chances of muscular hypertrophy.

Bodybuilding Reality

Q. I understand that increased work in a unit of time is the stimulus for muscle to grow. However, some of the exercises you've listed as having low-end Power Factors are the ones that make up the bulk of the chest and arm routines of professional bodybuilders. If these exercises were so ineffective, then how can they be responsible for putting that much muscle on the champions?

A. You assume that what you read in the bodybuilding magazines is true, that it is the exercises alone that contributed to the growth of the champions' muscles. As we've said before, the bodybuilding champions are the thoroughbreds of muscle; it's in their genes to have large muscles. They are huge because they're genetically predisposed to carry a large musculature on their frames, not because of their magic routines (for example, triple split, push/pull, intensity or insanity, up and down the rack, three days on, one day off, etc.) or their secret diet. It's time we all woke up to the fact that it's not in the genetic cards for all of us to be massive. Nor can we alter this fact by simply aping the training routine of a certain champion. In fact, the champion's training routine (particularly his precontest routine) would have about as much bearing on our attaining his muscle size as would our wearing the same shoes as he does, that is no effect whatsoever! Remember this: the first rule of success in bodybuilding is proper genetics. Without this, most of the other rules have no application. In fact, given the level of drugs that most of the champion bodybuilders take, probably very little of the rules that govern human physiology have much bearing, as the drugs serve to alter human physiology. When athletes take drugs, their muscles don't create the same amount of waste products, and they don't fatigue at the same rate. Drugs alter both processes of normal human physiology. Unless you're currently on steroids, regardless of the potential consequences, then you'll experience no gains in muscle mass by training like the champions. Muscular gains come when you train intelligently, which means observing and understanding the economics of growth and recovery.

Believe and Achieve

Q. I recently read an article in which a champion bodybuilder claimed that visualization was the key factor in building his body. If this were so, wouldn't it negate the need for any form of training at all?

A. Yes, it would. While the mind is certainly important, not only in bodybuilding but in all areas of human endeavor, and while confidence in yourself and having goals are also important, neither are the actual stimulus for building bigger and stronger muscles. To do this, the mind is important in making sure that you're motivated sufficiently to get your behind in the gym to train hard. While everyone appreciates a good metaphor, there is a proper time and a place for everything. Affirmations that involve phrases like "biceps like mountains" and "lats like manta rays" are entertaining, to be sure, but if you buy into these visualization pitches, then you've left the world of reality. We would be the last to tell you that if you are three foot two and have a face like Quasimodo and visualize that you're six foot six with blue eyes it will happen. The proponents of such irrational gibberish have terms to describe their techniques, like *mental imagery* or *visualization*, and it's rampant throughout bodybuilding. Statements like "Believe and achieve" adorn the back of many a personally inscribed weight belt. But the truth is, this is chicanery straight out of *The Flim Flam Man* and won't put another inch on your arms, no matter how Cartesianly clear and distinct your "visualization" processes about the size you want your muscles to become may be. The mind is important, in keeping you motivated to get into the gym and train intensely enough to stimulate your muscles to grow, which, as we have discussed in previous chapters, is not an easy activity to engage in. In fact, it's downright uncomfortable.

More on Genetics

Q. If genetics are so important—and mine aren't the same as the champion bodybuilders—am I wasting my time in training my physique?

A. If you're asking us if you should throw in the towel on your training because your genetics have revealed that you're not the spitting image of Conan the Barbarian, our answer is No! Just because you don't have the muscle bellies of an Arnold Schwarzenegger doesn't mean that you don't have the genetics of an equally impressive body when developed to the limits of your potential. After all, Steve Reeves, Arnold Schwarzenegger, Lee Haney, Lou Ferrigno, Bruce Lee, Evander Holyfield, and Michael Jordan don't have identical genetics either, yet they all have magnificent physiques. If you train *properly*, you can realize your own unique physiological potential, which may well supersede any of the bodybuilders you presently look up to. But as potential is simply the expression of a possibility, you'll never know what your physical potential is unless you train hard enough to realize it. So our advice is to get back in the gym and train smart.

Confusing Your Muscles

Q. I've read that since muscles adapt quickly to the stress of exercise, you've got to constantly change your exercises, sets, reps, and even training systems with great frequency in order to keep your muscles confused. The idea is if they are confused, they cannot become complacent; the constant change shocks your muscles into new spurts of growth. Is this true?

A. Certainly not from a scientific basis. Remember that muscle has only one function: contraction. This being the case, how could having it perform a different exercise be considered shock? If you decided one workout to "shock" your biceps muscle by having it perform a curl with a barbell instead of a dumbbell, it would still be performing its primary function, contraction, so where exactly would the shock come in? Likewise if instead of performing a dumbbell curl sitting up you decided to perform it lying back at a 45-degree angle, the primary function of the biceps muscle would still be carried out. From a scientific standpoint, you cannot shock, hoax, cajole, befuddle, or confuse a muscle into doing anything but contract.

Full-Range Training for Fuller Muscle Development
Q. For years machine companies like Nautilus have advocated the performance of full-range exercise in order to create a fuller muscle. In fact, their offset cams were said to be revolutionary. If I understand you correctly, you're saying that the Nautilus principles and their machines are unnecessary.

A. We've never said that machines like Nautilus are unnecessary. However, we've demonstrated that a full range of motion for building maximum strength has very little to no importance. Some machine companies would have you believe that if you performed full-range curls on one of their machines, the stress of the exercise would be more directly focused onto your "lower biceps" (then, of course, you would have to buy one of their other biceps machines in order to train the remaining portions of your biceps). This is ridiculous, particularly since muscle fibers, regardless of where they are located in a given muscle, are recruited by one thing and one thing only: the amount of weight that they are being made to contract against. If you want to ensure that all of the available muscle fibers in your biceps will be stimulated to grow bigger and stronger, then you have to employ a resistance that is heavy enough to recruit all of the available fibers. Excessive stretching and an exaggerated range of motion play no part at all in the muscle fiber recruitment process.

Shaping a Muscle
Q. I like to perform a heavy basic compound exercise for mass, a second movement for shape, and a third to bring out the definition or "quality" in my muscles. What's wrong with that?

A. Simply the fact that your very question is absolutely loaded with false assumptions. We quite agree that heavy basic compound movements are what are required to build muscle mass, but they are also the ones that bring out the inherent shape of your muscles and that burn away the most bodyfat, thus leading to a more "defined" state. Technically speaking, there is no such thing as a pure shaping or definition exercise. It is the burning of calories above what you eat in the form of calories that leads to definition. The more calories you expend, the greater the likelihood of your becoming defined. Therefore the exercises that burn the most calories on a per-set basis are also the ones that will lead to the creation of the greatest definition. And which exercises are these? The same ones you use to build maximum mass, heavy, basic, compound movements. In conclusion, you cannot train for shape or definition more successfully with isolation exercises than you can with compound exercises.

Tearing Down and Building Up
Q. For decades, many bodybuilding authors and even a few exercise physiologists have indicated that weight training "tears down the muscles" and that you should then take a few days off in order to allow the muscles to build back bigger and stronger. Is this actually what happens?

A. While it may sound plausible, in reality it just doesn't happen this way. Exercise performed for the express purpose of getting stronger should never "tear down" or damage the muscles. If it did, you wouldn't be able to leave the gym after an intense weight workout. Proper bodybuilding training is geared to stimulate growth, not cause cellular trauma. In other words, the workout acts as a trigger mechanism that sets into motion a series of physiological steps that will hopefully culminate in the production of muscle growth. This is providing certain conditions are met, such as time for complete recovery and growth and adequate nutrition. While there are some changes in muscle cell permeability as a result of an intense workout (for example, sometimes a leakage of certain enzymes through the cell membrane occurs), never should dramatic changes occur in the structural integrity of muscle fibers as a result of working out. "Tearing down" would constitute injury.

Train for a Pump
Q. I know many bodybuilders who say that "getting a good pump" is the only key to muscle growth stimulation. If this is so, then why all this talk of heavy weights?

A. Simply because it isn't so. There exists no evidence whatsoever that a "pump" is an index of muscle-growth stimulation. All bodybuilders achieve a pump to some degree every time they work out, yet, obviously, not all bodybuilders grow as a result of each workout. For that matter, people who perform high-volume exercise, such as cyclists, joggers, and even Stairmaster enthusiasts, also experience a pump but don't experience growth as a result. If the pump was the *sine qua non* of muscle-growth stimulation, then all of these high-volume exercisers would jump up in weight classes on a weekly basis. A pump is simply *edema*, the temporary swelling of tissue due to a fluid buildup, in this case blood, in the muscle being worked. Unless growth was stimulated as a result of a workout, however, once the pump subsides, the muscle will revert to its previous size. Strength training, which is what proper bodybuilding really is, doesn't always produce much in the way of a pump—but there can be no mistaking the fact that after a hard peak overload workout the body is about to undergo some profound physiological changes. And therein lies the only true key to muscle growth, as it was discovered a long, long time ago that muscular size and strength are directly related. More precisely, the strength of a muscle is proportional to its cross-sectional area. In other words, a stronger muscle is a bigger muscle. That's why when you remove a cast from a limb that's been immobilized due to injury, you notice that it's atrophied, or become smaller from disuse. What's the doctor's prescription for rehabilitating that limb, to get those muscles to grow bigger again? Strength training! And the stronger the limb becomes, the bigger it becomes. As a result, if you want to grow bigger and bigger muscles, you should always train with an eye toward a strength improvement. A pump, while a nice feeling admittedly, is not an accurate indicator of muscle-growth stimulation.

The Problem with Training More Frequently

Q. I see plenty of bodybuilders training six days a week—and they're huge. So why shouldn't I train every day if I want to?

A. Almost every professional bodybuilder is on some form of growth drug, which is what allows them to train so frequently without overtraining. However, growth drugs have dire side effects, which is why we adamantly oppose their use. We are concerned solely with the training requirements of human beings with normal human endocrinology, and what we've discovered is that nobody needs to train that frequently if making maximum gains in size and strength is your goal. Heavy-overload exercise—the only kind that results in immediate muscular adaptation—is a form of stress to the muscles and the overall physical system. When performed properly, such training will stimulate a compensatory buildup in the form of additional muscle size and strength, which aids the body in coping more successfully with similar stressors in the future. However, if you insist on training six to seven days a week (whether on a system of three days on, one day off or four days on, one day off), you'll see a decompensatory effect (i.e., an overtrained condition of weaker and smaller muscles), as the resulting drain on the regulatory subsystems of the body will actually prevent the buildup of muscle tissue. In fact, all of the energy reserves will have to be called upon simply to attempt to overcome the energy debt caused by such overtraining. These facts strongly indicate that the less time spent in the gym, the better your results will be.

Instinctive Training
Q. Don't the advanced bodybuilders rely on the "instinctive training" principle to make advanced gains?

A. Advanced bodybuilders rely on a good many things (many of them being illegal) to make advanced gains. However, attempting to monitor your results by such a subjective index as how you felt at a given time would, in the final analysis, yield you nothing. Only in bodybuilding could one postulate such a ludicrous hypothesis as "instinctive training" and get away with it. Could you imagine, for example, an Olympic sprinter trying to monitor his or her progress by feel or instinct, never measuring progress with a stopwatch, never having any objective measure of the effects of certain training techniques or of improvements from one month to the next? And yet this is exactly the kind of irrational, low-tech methodology that bodybuilders have always used. Feeling something to be true is no guarantee that it is true.

Muscles and Speed
Q. I'm told that if my muscles get bigger, I'll become slower. Is this true?

A. The speed of a body movement is dependent on two factors:

   (1) the strength of the muscles that are actually involved when performing a specific skill
   (2) your capacity to recruit muscle fibers while performing the movement (neurological efficiency)

It's wrong to assume that a muscle will slow down when its strength and size increase. The correlation between the speed of a muscle movement and the strength level of the muscle are positively related. Therefore, to increase the speed of a muscle movement, increase the strength levels of the muscles needed to perform that particular movement.

Muscle Turning to Fat
Q. If I build a lot of muscle mass, doesn't it all turn to fat when I get older?

A. This is perhaps the most common misconception about proper bodybuilding. Muscle can no more be turned into fat than an apple can be turned into an orange. They are two entirely different cells; one cannot become the other. If you were to chemically analyze fat and muscle, you would discover that muscle and fat both contain varying amounts of protein, water, lipids, and inorganic materials. However, when muscle is exercised, it contracts and produces movement, whereas fat will not contract and is usually stored in the body as a source of fuel. It is physiologically and chemically impossible to convert muscle to fat and vice versa. A simple explanation of what actually takes place can be illustrated by observing the ex-athlete's pattern of exercise and caloric intake. When an athlete stops training his or her muscles, the muscles will begin to atrophy, or shrink from disuse. At the same time, the athlete will continue to consume the same level of calories, more than are needed to maintain his or her bodyweight/ energy demands. The excess is then stored in the body as additional fat. If an athlete becomes obese after terminating a strength-training program, it is due to caloric imbalance (that is, taking in more than is being burned off), and not from muscle transforming to fat. Some individuals believe that their bodyweight should remain constant after the termination of a strength-training program. Unfortunately, these individuals fail to understand that if they lose ten pounds of muscle mass through muscle atrophy and their body weight remains the same, then the weight loss that is attributed to muscle atrophy has been replaced by deposits of additional fat. Thus, upon stopping training, an athlete should also alter his or her calorie intake.

Failure Plus Negatives Plus Static
Q. What about performing 1 set to failure followed by 1 negative followed by 1 static hold? I've heard several people recommend this, claiming they had good results.

A. I have no doubt that this technique will garner results. The difficulty I have with strategies like this is that I always want to know which of the three components is contributing the most to the growth process. We know that a training program of 1 set to failure will stimulate muscle growth. We also know that a program of negatives only will stimulate muscle growth, as will a program of only static holds. While we're on the subject, we know that pre-exhaustion, supersets, sets of 100, and so forth will also build muscle. So what would be your opinion of a program that counseled 1 set of 100, 1 superset, 1 pre-exhaustion, 1 set to failure, 1 negative, and 1 static hold? What would be your motivation for wanting to try a program like this? Are you interested in testing your tolerance to exercise? The fact is that any time you go into the gym, your body is capable of stimulating a certain amount of growth and no more (possibly less, but no more). So wouldn't you be interested in the most *efficient* way of getting that certain amount of growth?

Necessity of Full Range

Q. *Has there ever been a study proving that a full range of motion is necessary in order to stimulate muscle growth?*

A. No, and there never will be. It may seem as though we are recklessly predicting the outcome of future scientific experiments by saying that there never will be a study that proves a full range of motion is necessary to stimulate muscle growth. But we are certain about it. First of all, our own experience with static contractions and strong-range Power Factor Training revealed that exercising with 0 to 20 percent range of motion would stimulate substantial new muscle growth and strength increases. You cannot have one valid study that says 0 to 20 percent range will stimulate muscle growth and a second valid study that says only 100 percent range of motion will stimulate growth. Second, outside of the gym virtually none of the six billion people on the planet use a full range of motion when going about their daily activities, and yet these people are all able to increase their muscle mass. For example, climbing stairs will increase the strength in your legs even though taking a six-inch step is nowhere near a full range of leg motion. It is perfectly rational to conclude that there never will be a study that proves a full range of motion is a requirement for muscle growth, just as there will never be a study proving that eating kiwi is a requirement for muscle growth.

Mixing Cardio with Strength Training

Q. I want to gain muscle and lose fat. Can I mix cardio workouts with strength workouts and not overtrain?

A. This is one of the most common questions that we receive. The lack of good information on this subject still continues to amaze us. Aerobic training, to lose fat, is vastly different from efficient anaerobic training to gain strength. There is really no reason to abandon one in favor of the other. Aerobic training, by definition, is low intensity and of an extended duration. This means that if you are jogging on a treadmill, for example, you should be able to carry on a normal conversation with the person beside you. You should not be gasping for breath or otherwise exerting yourself at a rate that you cannot sustain for 20, 30, or 40 minutes. This type of low-intensity exercise has wonderfully beneficial effects on the heart and respiratory system but does virtually nothing to tax the skeletal muscles. It can always be argued that the body has a finite recovery capacity and that doing any exercise other than weight lifting will decrease your rate of progress. But we have yet to see a single person arrest his strength-training progress by performing proper aerobics three or four days per week.

Note that the progressive intensity that is critical to anaerobic strength training is not a required element of aerobic training. The inability to make this distinction causes some bodybuilders to engage in "progressive aerobics" that eventually see them donning forty-pound backpacks and running hills in order to outdo their last effort. That is not proper aerobic training. In aerobics it is entirely appropriate to adopt a program of, say, four 30-minute walks per week and then leave that program unchanged for twenty years. It's only when you turn your aerobic training into a high-intensity effort that it can begin to make any appreciable decrease in your rate of progress in strength training.

Strength Training vs. Size Training

Q. My strength has gone up from training, but my size has stayed the same. Should I be training differently?

A. The belief that there are separate ways to train for size and for strength is without any foundation in reality. There are many reasons why size gains do not manifest as quickly as strength gains. These reasons are due to the laws of both physiology and geometry. Think of it this way: if there was a method of training that delivered size gains without strength gains it would be possible to develop enormous muscle size but still lack the ability to lift even the lightest weight. Similarly, if there was a way to train that would develop tremendous strength but not in size, then it would be possible to squat 800 pounds and bench 500 pounds and have pencil-thin legs and arms. Obviously, this is not the way the human body functions. Muscle size and muscle strength share an exact correlation, and if you are getting appreciably stronger then your muscles are getting bigger—period. The single greatest tool in helping you realize that you are making both strength and size gains at the same time is a simple fat caliper or other bodyfat-measuring device. Using a combination of a bathroom scale and a fat caliper you will discover that as you get stronger your lean mass is increasing. Without the fat caliper you might discover that although you got stronger, your weight decreased by 5 pounds and your arms don't look or measure any bigger. But the truth may be that you've gained 10 pounds of muscle, lost 15 pounds of fat (much from your arms), and are actually making terrific progress. Take the time to apply some reason and science to your training, and you will be rewarded with the satisfaction of seeing your progress and staying motivated.

Periodization

Q. Much has been written in the muscle and powerlifting magazines about the importance of cycling your workout routines to prevent overtraining. They say that you have to do this in order to stress the muscles differently and "shock the muscles" back into growing again. They say that doing so gives the body a break from heavy workouts, which lead rapidly to overtraining. What is Power Factor Training's response to this?

A. The Power Factor Training response is the same as that of enlightened exercise physiologists: we reject the theory of cycling or "periodization," in which reducing overload and intensity and increasing the length and frequency of workouts are requisites for building muscular mass and strength. There's simply no evidence that engaging in activities that have been shown to have no effect on the process of hypertrophy will if scheduled a certain way somehow enhance the hypertrophy process. People who advocate periodization are ignorant of the fact that the sole stimulus for size and strength increases is workouts involving a huge muscular output (that is, Power Factor Training). Remember, in order for your body to alter its existing levels of muscle mass and strength, a demand has to be imposed upon your central nervous system that is so intense that it is perceived as potentially life-threatening by the body. Power Factor Training creates this demand better than any other method of training because of the weights employed and the superior overload imposed on the muscles. This is precisely what makes it so productive. The heavier the demand, the faster you grow. A properly conducted Power Factor Training routine also compensates for the stress on the body, because it's carried on only for brief periods and includes adequate time for recuperation and growth between workouts. Alternating periods of reducing your muscular overload and performing higher reps with periods of moderate intensity and performing moderate reps or any other such reduction in muscular output is an absolute waste of time. Knowing these facts regarding the requirements for muscle growth, there is no excuse for the serious bodybuilder or powerlifter to train with less than all-out effort each and every workout.

Comparing Numbers
Q. Can I compare my Power Factor and Power Index to someone else's?

A. The simple answer to your question is no, and the reason is that you can't compare individuals. There are many reasons for this, a few of which deserve some elaboration. Many bodybuilders and strength athletes refuse to believe that size and strength are related. To support this erroneous contention, they will invariably point to two individuals and note that one of them is smaller and less massive than the other one and yet can lift more weight. A contradiction? Only an apparent one. What they've failed to consider in their example is the fact that accurate comparisons between individuals like this cannot be made, as there exist just too many independent variables to consider. It may be true that the smaller individual has a sixteen-inch arm and can curl 150 pounds, while the larger one has a seventeen-inch arm and can curl only 135 pounds. The point to be made here is that the individual with the sixteen-inch arm will be stronger than he was when his arm has grown to seventeen inches because that size increase will be due to increased muscle strength. Likewise the bigger individual will be stronger than he was when his arm measures nineteen inches. In some instances, the variance in strength can be due to leverage differences. For example, the smaller arm has shorter bones in it and thus lifts the weight a shorter distance, thereby providing the smaller individual with a decided advantage in demonstrating strength. Another contributing factor could be the existence of favorable attachment points. For example, if one individual's biceps tendon is attached further down his forearm from the elbow (and this is an atypical placement, admittedly), then this individual will have a pronounced leverage advantage. The outstanding feature of partials, however, is that they serve as a great equalizer in that both individuals will be overloading their respective muscles while they are in the structurally most advantageous (and strongest) position. Another factor influencing strength development is neuromuscular efficiency. A cubic inch of one individual's muscle may be capable of producing more power than a comparable amount of another individual's. Because of these and other differences between individuals, meaningful comparisons are difficult to make. Comparisons are best made only by a bodybuilder's measuring himself over a given period of time.

Sometimes you can handle super-heavy weights more comfortably when lying on the floor than when lying on a flat bench.

Power Factor's Effectiveness
Q. Why is Power Factor Training more effective than other forms of training?

A. Power Factor Training is the most effective training method simply because it delivers the highest overload to the muscles. Plain and simple, with Power Factor Training you use your mind to guide your progress. If you study our species' history, you will see that in all fields of endeavor, whether it is philosophy, science, engineering, medicine, architecture, bodybuilding, or anything else, the greatest strides have invariably resulted from the application of our faculty of reason. And when this faculty is brought to bear on the science of exercise, specifically the cause-and-effect relationship of overload on muscular size and strength, it becomes immediately apparent that the most productive training system will be the one that employs the greatest overload to the muscles. Whichever method delivers this maximum overload will trigger the greatest adaptive response from the body in the form of muscular overcompensation. Further, the method must also take into account the physiologic principles of recovery and growth after this overload has been applied. When these two aspects of training have been followed, the net gain is always progressive and superior results. It further stands to reason that the most productive training method for our species to utilize in its quest for super strength and massive muscles is Power Factor Training. This doesn't mean that all other training methods are bad, nor that unless you use Power Factor Training you're doomed to failure. Conventional training methods deliver some results, because they do provide some form of progressive overload to the muscles. However, what they don't provide is maximum overload to the muscles and a precise, mathematical method of gauging both muscular output and progress. Only Power Factor Training provides these. We're not naive enough to expect Power Factor Training to entirely replace conventional training methods. After all, the airplane didn't entirely replace the ocean liner and train as modes of transportation either. However, there can be no dispute about which will get you to your destination quicker.

Tendons and Ligaments
Q. I'm a bodybuilder, and while I like to lift heavy weights, I'm wondering what difference developing strong ligament strength in addition to muscle strength will have on my physique.

A. To get the most out of your Power Factor Training, you should never neglect the exercises that build the strength of the connective tissue and that accustom the body to handling extremely heavy poundages. The only way to obtain this power is through handling the heaviest possible poundages over short ranges of muscle action and, obviously, through the utilization of exercises that work the largest muscle groups of the body such as the thighs, the back, shoulders, chest, and arms. In addition to increasing overall strength and mass and toning up the muscles and connective tissue, Power Factor Training also increases confidence and enthusiasm. By handling extremely heavy poundages, you develop a positive mental outlook and sense of achievement, and the poundages you used in ordinary movements that seemed so heavy will seem as light as a feather after your Power Factor Training (should you decide to return to conventional training, that is!).

Champion Genetics
Q. If I engage in Power Factor Training, will I become a champion bodybuilder?

A. There are many factors to consider when answering your question, not the least of which is genetics. As an example, no one would dispute that you'd need to be tall to be a successful professional basketball player (all Spud Webbs notwithstanding) or short to be a professional jockey. It's also obvious that bouncing a basketball or running up and down a court won't make you any taller, and riding a horse all day long won't make you shorter. Your height is determined by your genetics. Genetics also play a role in the success or failure of champion bodybuilders, namely their genetic potential to develop inordinately large muscles. Two of the more important factors in determining a muscle's size potential is the length of a given muscle from the tendon attachments on each end and the fiber density of the muscle itself. The longer the muscle, the greater the cross-sectional area when contracted and thus the greater volume that muscle has the potential to reach. If you have extremely long muscle bellies (i.e., length, width, low insertion point, etc.) throughout your entire physique, Power Factor Training will help you realize all of your genetic potential and if you also have the mental discipline you could well become a champion.

Too Old to Train
Q. I'm very interested in increasing my power and muscle mass. However, I'm over fifty years of age and hon-

estly believe that I am too old to benefit from Power Factor Training. Is there another activity that you can recommend for old-timers like me?

A. While we empathize with your concerns about returning to training after a lengthy layoff, we do not at all agree with your conclusion. In fact, a University of Southern California study involving a group of seventy-year-old men showed significant improvement in muscular strength after an eight-week strength-training program. You're never too old to start strength training. Remember that bigger muscles are stronger muscles and stronger muscles contribute to any movement activity, improve posture, and elevate your metabolism, which allows you to burn bodyfat more efficiently and helps to prevent injuries. Stronger muscles also mean more stable joints, which are usually the first areas to lose support and suffer pain as we get older. With regard to your question regarding another activity, we're inclined to recommend Power Factor Training. Not only are your joints, muscles, and connective tissue strengthened by proper Power Factor Training, but it produces benefits in a third of the time than, say, walking or swimming. Regardless of your age, if you can move a limb even a couple of inches, then you can move it against resistance and stimulate your muscles to grow stronger. However, be sure your physician gives you the OK before resuming any vigorous exercise program.

Strength vs. Speed

Q. Even though I believe what you said about a stronger athlete being a better athlete, I'm not sure that a stronger athlete makes a faster athlete. I need speed in my sport, martial arts. Will Power Factor Training be able to deliver it?

A. Absolutely! A stronger athlete is a faster athlete precisely because of the increased strength factor. Let's say you want to press a 100-pound barbell overhead as fast as possible. If your deltoids, traps, and triceps muscles are capable of combining to press 102 pounds, then your speed of movement with 100 pounds will obviously be very slow. It might even take 5 or 6 seconds to move the weight to the locked-out position. On the other hand, if the involved muscles are capable of pressing 200 pounds, you'll be able to press the 100-pound barbell in a ½ second and maybe even less time. If your pressing ability is 250 pounds, then your speed of movement will be even more rapid. As skill is not significantly involved in pressing a barbell, the increase in speed is obviously due to the strengthening of the muscles. If all else is equal, the stronger individual will also move the fastest, as he or she will have the greatest muscle mass to bodyweight ratio. After all, if you add more horsepower to the engine of an automobile, it will move faster.

Leaner and Stronger

Q. Don't you think you're stronger when you're heavier, even though that extra bodyweight isn't all muscle?

A. No, absolutely not. In fact, rather than helping body strength, any excess fat actually hinders body strength. Some studies performed on overweight individuals have revealed that intramuscular fat (which is fat found in between muscle fibers) actually hinders the process of muscular contraction, as it serves to create intercellular friction. This has the effect of making you weaker than you would be if your cells were unobstructed. In other words, the leaner you are, the stronger you are.

Training for Size and Strength Only

Q. Can you develop much in the way of cardiovascular fitness from Power Factor Training?

A. Not really. When you are employing high-intensity Power Factor Training, you are doing so specifically for muscular mass and strength increases. You can train specifically for muscular mass or specifically for cardiovascular fitness, but both require distinct forms of training to achieve. A concept in exercise physiology known as *specificity* states that a certain type of training effort will bring about a certain type of training effect. If you want to develop a high degree of cardiovascular fitness, than you have to perform a great amount of highly repetitive, low-intensity training. Power Factor Training, because of its high-intensity nature, does not build the type of cardiovascular fitness that specific aerobic training does. Jogging, cycling, and swimming are the kinds of activities that we're referring to. You can of course develop a little cardiovascular fitness from your workouts because any type of exercise involves the heart and circulatory system to some degree. In this respect, it is possible to divide the concept of specificity in two by training for some muscular mass and some cardiovascular fitness each time you work out. But in order to reach the uppermost limits of your potential in either of these two categories, you must specifically train for that category. If building muscular mass and strength as quickly as possible is your goal, then you must train specifically for such increases and give it 100 percent of your effort and focus. If you want to gain as much cardiovascular fitness as you can, then train with 100 percent of your effort for that. Don't divide it in two during strength training workouts.

What to Expect

Q. How much muscle mass can you expect to build in one year of Power Factor Training?

A. It's been said that if you are lucky enough to gain 10 pounds of muscle in one year then you can consider yourself most fortunate. However, in light of the results we've been seeing in Power Factor Training, that may now be inaccurate. For example, in one week of Power Factor Training, one of the authors of this book, John Little, gained 15 pounds after having remained at a bodyweight of 180 pounds for more than ten years. Did he eat more and train less during that week, thereby gaining 15 pounds of fat? No. He didn't alter his diet in any way and his waist size remained the same while his Power Factor and Power Index went up dramatically, which indicated a pronounced increase in strength. The only reason for the increase then was the adaptive bodily response (that is, muscular overcompensation) to the superior overload imposed on it in his Power Factor Training. Little put on an additional 10 pounds over the next four weeks (twelve workouts) as his Power Factor and Power Index increased on a per-workout basis. Perhaps, however, for the majority of trainees who still cling to less-intense methods of training, 10 pounds a year is a more realistic expectation, at least during the first few years. If you think that 10 pounds per year isn't much (especially in light of the high-set, seven-days-per-week training methods most bodybuilders employ), then just imagine how little it actually is when measured on a day-to-day basis. With 365 days in a year, the daily amount of muscle growth amounts to only 0.027 pound, which is less than .5 ounce. That's not even enough to register on a bodyweight scale! With Power Factor Training the trainees make palpable, measurable progress on a consistent basis, and as evidenced by Little's success, it's not uncommon to gain upward of 15 pounds in under a month.

As always, train smart!

Peter Sisco and John Little

Index

Aerobic training, 233
Age, 238–39
Alpha strength, 20–21, 24
  biceps workouts for, 184–85
  chest workouts for, 172–75
  forearm workouts for, 186–87
  triceps workouts for, 179–82
Anaerobic training, 233
Anderson, Paul, 37
Anterior deltoids, exercises for
  barbell bench press, 60–61, 134
  bilateral high pulley cable crossover,
    58, 132
  close-grip bench press, 76–77, 145
  decline barbell bench press, 59, 133
  dumbbell fly, 50–51, 128
  flat bench cable crossover, 48–49, 127
  Hammer Strength dip machine,
    78–79, 146
  incline barbell press, 52–53, 128–29
  Nautilus 10-degree chest machine, 54–55,
    129–30
  unilateral high pulley cable crossover,
    56–57, 130–31
Arm exercises
  bent-over dumbbell triceps extension
    (triceps kickback), 69, 141
  close-grip bench press, 76–77, 145
  Hammer Strength dip machine,
    78–79, 146
  Hammer Strength machine biceps curl,
    96–97, 156
  high pulley pressdown, 64–65, 137–38
  lying dumbbell curl, 84–85, 150
  lying low pulley triceps curl, 66–67, 139
  Nautilus machine curl, 85, 151
  Nautilus triceps machine, 68, 140
  rating methods/procedures, 122–24
  seated barbell curls, 100–101, 158
  seated barbell reverse wrist curl,
    112–13, 164
  seated barbell triceps extension,
    74–75, 144
  seated barbell wrist curl, 116–17, 166
  seated dumbbell curl, 94–95, 155
  seated dumbbell reverse wrist curl,
    114–15, 165
  seated dumbbell wrist curl, 118, 167
  seated low pulley reverse wrist curl,
    104–5, 160
  seated low pulley wrist curl, 106–7, 161
  seated Scott barbell curl, 88–89, 153
  seated Scott dumbbell curl, 82–83, 149
  standing barbell curl, 98–99, 157

standing barbell reverse curl, 110–11, 163
standing barbell triceps extension,
  72–73, 143
standing barbell wrist curl behind back,
  119, 168
standing dumbbell curl, 92–93, 154
standing dumbbell reverse curl,
  108–9, 162
standing low pulley curl, 80–81, 148
standing one-arm dumbbell triceps extension (triceps curl), 70, 142
standing Scott barbell curl, 90–91, 154
standing Scott dumbbell curl, 86–87, 152
Arm muscles
  biceps, 80
  forearm, 102–3
  triceps, 64
  workouts for, 179–88
Atherton, John "Jack," 20, 21

Back exercises. See Upper back muscles,
  exercises for
Barbell bench press, 60–61, 134
Belts, weight-lifting, 220–21
Bench press(es), 37
  barbell, 60–61, 134
  close-grip, 76–77, 145
  decline barbell, 59, 133
Benefits of Power Factor Training, 2–4
Bent-over dumbbell triceps extension (triceps
  kickback), 69, 141
Beta strength, 20–21, 25–26
  biceps workouts for, 185–86
  chest workouts for, 175–78
  forearm workouts for, 188
  triceps workouts for, 182–83
Biceps (biceps brachii), 80
  comparisons of exercises for, 159
  exercises for
    Hammer Strength machine biceps
      curl, 96–97, 156
    lying dumbbell curl, 84–85, 150
    Nautilus machine curl, 85, 151
    seated barbell curls, 100–101, 158
    seated dumbbell curl, 94–95, 155
    seated Scott barbell curl, 88–89, 153
    seated Scott dumbbell curl, 82–83, 149
    standing barbell curl, 98–99, 157
    standing barbell reverse curl,
      110–11, 163
    standing dumbbell curl, 92–93, 154
    standing low pulley curl, 80–81, 148
    standing Scott barbell curl,
      90–91, 154

standing Scott dumbbell curl,
  86–87, 152
high alpha strength workouts for, 184–85
high beta strength workouts for, 185–86
Bilateral high pulley cable crossover, 58, 132
Bodybuilding
  conventional vs. Power Factor Training,
    6–8, 32–33
  and drugs, 229
  and genetic predisposition, 224–26, 238
  phases of, 39–41
  Sisco's laws of, 24–26
  and visualization, 225–26
Bodyweight
  and diet, 219–20
  and strength, 240
Brachialis, exercises for
  seated barbell reverse wrist curl,
    112–13, 164
  seated Scott dumbbell curl, 82–83, 149
  standing barbell reverse curl, 110–11, 163
  standing dumbbell reverse curl,
    108–9, 162
  standing low pulley curl, 80–81, 148
Brzycki, Matt, 29

Caloric intake, 219–20
Cardiovascular fitness
  and Power Factor Training, 240–41
  training for, 233
Cheating, 223–24
Chest
  exercises for, 44–61
    barbell bench press, 60–61, 134
    bilateral high pulley cable crossover,
      58, 132
    decline barbell bench press, 59, 133
    dumbbell fly, 50–51, 128
    flat bench cable crossover, 48–49, 127
    incline barbell press, 52–53, 128–29
    Nautilus machine pullover, 46–47,
      125–27
    Nautilus 10-degree chest machine,
      54–55, 129–30
    Power Factor comparisons, 135
    rating methods/procedures, 122–24
    straight-arm pullover, 45, 124–25
    unilateral high pulley cable crossover,
      56–57, 130–31
  high alpha strength workouts for, 172–75
  high beta strength workouts for, 175–78
  muscles of, 43–44
Clark, Anthony, 20, 21, 37
Close-grip bench press, 76–77, 145

Columbu, Franco, 221–22
Confusing your muscles, 226–27
Conventional training, Power Factor
          Training vs., 6–8, 32–33
Crossover(s)
          bilateral high pulley, 58, 132
          bilateral high pulley cable, 58, 132
          flat bench, 48–49, 127
          flat bench cable, 48–49, 127
          unilateral high pulley, 56–57, 130–31
          unilateral high pulley cable, 56–57,
                    130–31
Curl(s)
          Hammer Strength machine biceps,
                    96–97, 156
          lying dumbbell, 84–85, 150
          lying low pulley triceps, 66–67, 139
          Nautilus machine, 85, 151
          seated barbell, 100–101, 158
          seated barbell reverse wrist, 112–13, 164
          seated barbell wrist, 116–17, 166
          seated dumbbell, 94–95, 155
          seated dumbbell reverse wrist, 114–15, 165
          seated dumbbell wrist, 118, 167
          seated low pulley reverse wrist, 160
          seated low pulley wrist, 106–7, 161
          seated pulley reverse wrist, 104–5
          seated Scott barbell, 88–89, 153
          seated Scott dumbbell, 82–83, 149
          standing barbell, 98–99, 157
          standing barbell reverse, 110–11, 163
          standing barbell wrist, behind back,
                    119, 168
          standing dumbbell, 92–93, 154
          standing dumbbell reverse forearms,
                    108–9, 162
          standing low pulley, 80–81, 148
          standing one-arm dumbbell triceps, 70
          standing one-arm dumbbell triceps
                    extension, 142
          standing Scott barbell, 90–91, 154
          standing Scott dumbbell, 86–87, 152

Darden, Ellington, 28, 29
De Vries, Herbert A., 28
Decline barbell bench press, 59, 133
Definition, muscle, 222–23, 227–28
Deltoids, 44. *See also* Anterior deltoids,
          exercises for; Medial deltoids,
          exercises for
Dickerson, Chris, 221–22
Diet
          and muscle definition, 222–23
          and training changes, 231
          and weight loss, 219–20
Dip machine, Hammer Strength, 78–79, 146
Dorsal deep group muscles, 103
Drugs, 229
Dumbbell fly, 50–51, 128
Duration, intensity vs., 24, 27

Effectiveness
          of biceps exercises, 159
          of chest exercises, 135

of failure plus negatives plus static,
          231–32
of forearm exercises, 169
of full- vs. strongest-range training, 37–39
measuring, 4–6, 7–8, 12–14
muscle soreness and, 216–18
overload and, 12
and phases of training, 39
of Power Factor Training, 237
Sisco's laws for, 24–26
time and resistance as factors in, 34–37
of triceps exercises, 147
Exercise/workout performance record, 204
Extension(s)
          bent-over dumbbell triceps (triceps kick-
                    back), 69, 141
          seated barbell triceps, 74–75, 144
          standing barbell triceps, 72–73, 143
          standing one-arm dumbbell triceps
                    (triceps curl), 70, 142
Extensors. *See* Forearm extensors, exercises for

Failure
          exercising to, 122–23, 231–32
          and forced repetitions, 218
Fat
          and muscle mass, 231
          and strength, 240
Ferrigno, Lou, 37, 226
Flat bench cable crossover, 48–49, 127
Flexors. *See* Forearm flexors, exercises for
Fly, dumbbell. *See* Dumbbell fly
Forced repetitions, 218
Forearm extensors, exercises for
          seated dumbbell reverse wrist curl,
                    114–15, 165
          seated low pulley reverse wrist curl,
                    104–5, 160
Forearm flexors, exercises for
          Hammer Strength machine biceps curl,
                    96–97, 156
          lying dumbbell curl, 84–85, 150
          Nautilus machine curl, 85, 151
          seated barbell curls, 100–101, 158
          seated barbell reverse wrist curl,
                    112–13, 164
          seated barbell wrist curl, 116–17, 166
          seated dumbbell curl, 94–95, 155
          seated dumbbell wrist curl, 118, 167
          seated low pulley wrist curl, 106–7, 161
          seated Scott barbell curl, 88–89, 153
          seated Scott dumbbell curl, 82–83, 149
          standing barbell curl, 98–99, 157
          standing barbell reverse curl, 110–11, 163
          standing barbell wrist curl behind back,
                    119, 168
          standing dumbbell curl, 92–93, 154
          standing dumbbell reverse curl, 108–9, 162
          standing low pulley curl, 80–81, 148
          standing Scott barbell curl, 90–91, 154
          standing Scott dumbbell curl, 86–87, 152
Forearm muscles (antibrachial), 102–3
          dorsal group, 102–3
          volar group, 102

Forearms
          comparisons of exercises for, 169
          exercises for
                    seated barbell reverse wrist curl,
                              112–13, 164
                    standing barbell reverse curl,
                              110–11, 163
          high alpha strength workouts for, 186–87
          high beta strength workouts for, 188
Frequency of training, 26, 229–30
Full-range training
          and exercise machines, 227
          and muscle growth, 232
          strongest-range training vs., 32–33,
                    37–39, 215–16

Genetics, 224–26, 238
Goldberg, Dr. Alfred, 35
The Golfer's Two-Minute Workout, 122
Graphs, progress, 197–99
*Grow: A 28-Day Crash Course for Getting
          Huge* (Ellington Darden), 29
Growth, muscle. *See* Hypertrophy
Guinness Book of Records, 20

Hammer Strength machines
          actual vs. expected weights on, 146
          biceps curl, 96–97, 156
          dip machine, 78–79, 146
Hand muscles, 103–4
Haney, Lee, 226
Heavy Duty II: Mind and Body (Mike
          Mentzer), 29
High pulley pressdown, 64–65, 137–38
Holyfield, Evander, 226
Hypertrophy
          and Power Factor Training, 211–12
          stimulating muscles to, 34–37

Incline barbell press, 52–53, 128–29
Individuals, comparisons between,
          235–36
Injuries, 228
          and range of motion, 32
          and workout pace, 21
Instinctive training, 230
Intensity, 123
          and aerobic training, 233
          in bilateral high pulley cable crossover
                    exercise, 132
          of dumbbell fly exercises, 128
          duration vs., 27
          momentary, 24
          and muscle growth, 34–37
          and results, 208
          volumetric, 24–26

Jordan, Michael, 226
Journal of Physiology, 31

Kazmaier, Bill, 20, 21, 37

Lange, H., 34–35
Latissimus dorsi, 44

Latissimus dorsi, exercises for
    barbell bench press, 60–61, 134
    close-grip bench press, 76–77, 145
    Hammer Strength dip machine,
        78–79, 146
    Nautilus machine pullover, 46–47, 125–27
    straight-arm pullover, 45, 124–25
Lee, Bruce, 226
Lengthening muscles, 221–22
Ligaments, 237–38
Lying dumbbell curl, 84–85, 150
Lying low pulley triceps curl, 66–67, 139

Machines, actual vs. expected weight on,
    125–27, 129, 140, 146
Measurement
    of effectiveness, 4–6, 7–8, 12–14
    of intensity, 24–26
    of strength, 19, 20–21
    of weight on exercise machines, 125–27,
        129, 140, 146
Medial deltoids, exercises for
    barbell bench press, 60–61, 134
    close-grip bench press, 76–77, 145
    decline barbell bench press, 59, 133
    dumbbell fly, 50–51, 128
    Hammer Strength dip machine,
        78–79, 146
    incline barbell press, 52–53, 128–29
    Nautilus 10-degree chest machine, 54–55,
        129–30
Mental imagery, 225
Mentzer, Mike, 29–30, 37
Milo of Crotona, 34
Mistakes in Power Factor Training, 207–8
Momentary intensity, 24
Muscle mass, 214, 241
Muscles. *See also* Hypertrophy
    biceps, 80
    chest, 43–44
    confusing for growth, 226–27
    defining, 222–23
    and fat, 231
    forearm, 102–3
    genetics and size of, 238
    growth of, as training phase, 39–41
    lengthening, 221–22
    shaping, 227–28
    and speed, 230–31
    tearing of, 27–28
    triceps, 64
Muscular overload, 2

Nautilus machines, 227
    actual vs. expected weights on, 125, 129,
        140, 151
    curls on, 85, 151
    pullovers on, 46–47, 125–27
    10-degree chest machine, 54–55, 129–30
    triceps machine, 68, 140
Negatives, 231–32
*New High-Intensity Bodybuilding for
    Massive Muscles Fast* (Ellington
    Darden), 29

Overload, 2, 11–12, 24, 26, 34, 123
Overtraining, 8, 41, 219, 229–30

Partials, strong-range, 32, 37–39
Pectoralis major, 44
Pectoralis minor, 44
Pectorals, exercises for
    barbell bench press, 60–61, 134
    bilateral high pulley cable crossover,
        58, 132
    close-grip bench press, 76–77, 145
    decline barbell bench press, 59, 133
    dumbbell fly, 50–51, 128
    flat bench cable crossover, 48–49, 127
    Hammer Strength dip machine,
        78–79, 146
    incline barbell press, 52–53, 128–29
    Nautilus machine pullover, 46–47, 125–27
    Nautilus 10-degree chest machine, 54–55,
        129–30
    straight-arm pullover, 45, 124–25
    unilateral high pulley cable crossover,
        56–57, 130–31
Percentage of change, tracking, 192
Periodization, 234–35
Petow, H., 35
*The Physiology of Exercise for Physical
    Education and Athletics*
    (Herbert A. de Vries), 28
Power, forms of, 19–21
Power Factor Training, 121
    and age, 238–39
    benefits of, 2–4
    and cardiovascular fitness, 240–41
    and connective tissue, 237–38
    conventional training vs., 6–8, 32–33
    effectiveness of, 237
    frequency of training, 208
    full- vs. strongest-range, 215–16, 219
    mistakes made in, 207–8
    mixed results in, 208–9
    and muscle mass, 214, 241
    muscular mass building with, 211–12
    and other strength training, 208
    and overtraining, 218–19
    and perceived level of stimulation, 216–18
    and periodization, 234–35
    and range of motion, 232
    and recovery time, 200, 214–15
    repetitions in, 218–19
    sets and reps in, 212–13
    strongest range, finding, 210
    super-slow reps in, 210–11
    "sweet spot" for, 16–18
    weight choice for, 208, 213–14
*Power Factor Training: A Scientific
    Approach to Building Lean
    Muscle Mass*, 5
Power Factors
    analyzing by, 12–14
    for biceps exercises, 159
    for chest exercises, 135
    comparing, among individuals, 235–36
    definition of, 12

    determining, 5
    and failure rate measurement, 122–23
    for forearm exercises, 169
    formula for, 20
    and full- vs. strongest-range training,
        37–39
    increasing, 21, 23
    measurements using full-range techniques,
        44–45
    measuring intensity with, 24, 26
    planning workouts using, 195–96
    rating workouts by, 23
    and recovery time, 31–32, 200
    for triceps exercises, 147
Power Index
    comparing, among individuals, 235–36
    definition of, 21
    formula for, 20
    increasing, 23
    measuring intensity with, 25–26
    rating workouts by, 23
    and recovery time, 200
A Practical Approach to Strength Training
    (Matt Brzycki), 29
Press, incline barbell, 52–53, 128–29
Pressdown, high pulley, 64–65, 137–38
Progress, tracking. *See* Tracking progress
Progress graph, 197–99
Pronator teres, exercises for
    seated barbell reverse wrist curl,
        112–13, 164
    standing barbell reverse curl, 110–11, 163
    standing dumbbell reverse curl,
        108–9, 162
Pulleys, and actual weight lifted, 125–27, 130
Pullover(s)
    Nautilus machine, 46–47, 125–27
    straight-arm, 45, 124–25
Pump, and muscle growth, 228–29

Quadratus, exercises for
    seated barbell reverse wrist curl,
        112–13, 164
    standing barbell reverse curl, 110–11, 163

Range of motion, 121, 232
    and barbell curl effectiveness, 157–58
    full vs. strongest, 32–33
    strongest, 210
Ratings
    arm exercises, 137–69
    chest exercises, 121–36
    of workouts, 4–6, 23
Recovery, 26–32
    localized vs. systemic, 208–9
    in Power Factor Training, 214–15
    in training process, 39–40
    understanding, 200–202
Reeves, Steve, 226
Repetitions (reps)
    forced, 218
    and Power Factor Training, 212–13
    in relation to weight, 15–18
    super-slow, 210–11

Reserve strength, 19–20
Resistance, and effectiveness of exercise, 34–37
Roux, W., 34

Scapula, 44
Schedules, training, 27–32
Schwarzenegger, Arnold, 226
Scott, Larry, 222
Seated barbell curls, 100–101, 158
Seated barbell reverse wrist curl, 112–13, 164
Seated barbell triceps extension, 74–75, 144
Seated barbell wrist curl, 116–17, 166
Seated dumbbell curl, 94–95, 155
Seated dumbbell reverse wrist curl, 114–15, 165
Seated dumbbell wrist curl, 118, 167
Seated low pulley reverse wrist curl, 104–5, 160
Seated low pulley wrist curl, 106–7, 161
Seated Scott barbell curl, 88–89, 153
Seated Scott dumbbell curl, 82–83, 149
Serratus, exercises for
    bilateral high pulley cable crossover, 58, 132
    decline barbell bench press, 59, 133
    Nautilus machine pullover, 46–47, 125–27
    Nautilus 10-degree chest machine, 54–55, 129–30
    unilateral high pulley cable crossover, 56–57, 130–31
Serratus anterior (serratus magnus), 44
Sets and reps, in Power Factor Training, 212–13
Shaping muscles, 227–28
Shoulder, 44
Siebert, W. W., 35
Sisco's laws of bodybuilding, 24–26
Size training, strength training vs., 233–34
Soreness, as indicator of effectiveness, 216–18
Specialization, advantage of, 8–9
Specificity, 240
Speed
    and muscle size, 230–31
    strength vs., 239–40
Standing barbell curl, 98–99, 157
Standing barbell reverse curl, 110–11, 163
Standing barbell triceps extension, 72–73, 143
Standing barbell wrist curl behind back, 119, 168
Standing dumbbell curl, 92–93, 154
Standing dumbbell reverse curl, 108–9, 162
Standing low pulley curl, 80–81, 148
Standing one-arm dumbbell triceps extension (triceps curl), 70, 142
Standing Scott barbell curl, 90–91, 154
Standing Scott dumbbell curl, 86–87, 152
Static, 231–32

Static Contraction Training, 121
Static contraction workouts, 122
"Sticking points," 224
Stimulation, and muscle growth, 34–37
Straight-arm pullover, 45, 124–25
Strength
    and bodyweight, 240
    forms of, 19–21
    measurement of, 19–20
    measuring, with Power Index/Power Factor, 21–24
    speed vs., 239–40
Strength training
    aerobic training vs., 233
    size training vs., 233–34
Strength Training Principles: How to Get the Most Out of Your Workouts (Ellington Darden), 28
Strongest range of motion, 121, 210
Strongest-range training, full-range training vs., 32–33, 37–39, 215–16
Strong-range partials, 32
Subclavius, 44
"Sweet spot," 16–18, 213

Tearing, muscle, 27–28, 228
Tendons, 237–38
Teres major, 44
Tracking progress, 191–202
    graph for, 197–99
    percentage of change, 192
    performance records for, 203–4
    planning workouts, 195–97
    recovery time, 200–202
    workout record form for, 192–95
Training
    aerobic vs. strength, 233
    conventional vs. Power Factor, 6–8
    frequency of, 26, 229–30
    full- vs. strongest-range, 32, 37–39
    instinctive, 230
    phases of, 39–41
    schedules for, 27–32
    size vs. strength, 233–34
Trapezius, 44
Triceps
    comparisons of exercises, 147
    exercises for
        barbell bench press, 60–61, 134
        bent-over dumbbell triceps extension (triceps kickback), 69, 141
        close-grip bench press, 76–77, 145
        decline barbell bench press, 59, 133
        Hammer Strength dip machine, 78–79, 146
        high pulley pressdown, 64–65, 137–38
        incline barbell press, 52–53, 128–29
        lying low pulley triceps curl, 66–67, 139

Nautilus triceps machine, 68, 140
    seated barbell triceps extension, 74–75, 144
    standing barbell triceps extension, 72–73, 143
    standing one-arm dumbbell triceps extension (triceps curl), 70, 142
    straight-arm pullover, 45, 124–25
high alpha strength workouts for, 179–82
high beta strength workouts for, 182–83
Triceps kickback, 69, 141
True ribs, 44

Unilateral high pulley cable crossover, 56–57, 130–31
Upper back muscles, exercises for
    barbell bench press, 60–61, 134
    close-grip bench press, 76–77, 145
    Hammer Strength dip machine, 78–79, 146

Visualization, 225–26
Volar deep group muscles, 102
Volar superficial group muscles, 102
Volumetric intensity, 24–26

Weight-lifting belts, 220–21
Weight(s)
    body. *See* Bodyweight
    choice of, 208
    on machines, 125–27, 129, 140, 146
    in Power Factor Training, 213
    and repetitions, 15–18
Workouts
    aerobic vs. strength, 233
    biceps
        high alpha strength, 184–85
        high beta strength, 185–86
    cheating in, 223–24
    chest
        high alpha strength, 172–75
        high beta strength, 175–78
    forearms
        high alpha strength, 186–87
        high beta strength, 188
    frequency of, 189, 208, 229–30
    performance records for, 203–4
    and periodization, 234–35
    planning, 195–97
    progress graphs for, 197–99
    ratings of, 4–6, 23
    record form for, 192–95
    triceps
        high alpha strength, 179–82
        high beta strength, 182–83
    variety in, 226–27

Yates, Dorian, 37